DEVOTIONAL

AMAZING
Grace

BELLE
CITY
GIFTS

BroadStreet Publishing Group LLC
Savage, Minnesota
Broadstreetpublishing.com

Amazing Grace DEVOTIONAL

978-1-4245-6001-1

Design by Chris Garborg | garborgdesign.com

Edited and compiled by Michelle Winger | literallyprecise.com

Printed in China.

20   21   22   23   24   25   7   6   5   4   3   2   1

INTRODUCTION

The circumstances of life may have you feeling overwhelmed, frustrated, or discouraged. Because God's love for you is unchanging and his promises are true, you can choose to believe in the steady outpouring of grace he has for you each day.

Find the hope, joy, and strength that is abundant in God as you reflect on these devotional entries, Scriptures, and prayers. Be inspired as you record what's on your heart in the space provided.

Claim God's grace over your life and continue to believe that your Creator loves you deeply and is with you always no matter what comes your way.

ALL THINGS NEW

He who sat on the throne said, "Behold, I make all things new.
" And He said to me, "Write, for these words are true and faithful."
REVELATION 21:5 NKJV

The most beautiful thing about the God we've entrusted our lives to is that he makes all things new. That is a faithful statement—it has always been true and will always be true.

As we begin a new year, empty and full of both bright promise and worrisome unknown, we can rest our souls in the truth that our God will make everything new. Our regrets, mistakes, and failures are nothing compared to his covenanted promise of redemption and newness.

How do you see God making all things new in your life?

NEW EVERY MORNING

The steadfast love of the Lord never ceases,
his mercies never come to an end;
they are new every morning;
great is your faithfulness.

LAMENTATIONS 3:22-23 NRSV

It is beautiful to know that the mercies of our God are new every single morning. To know that the grace we spent on yesterday will still be abundant enough for the troubles we will face today. To know that his faithfulness is true even when we wander, and his love is steadfast even when ours fails.

We don't deserve the mercy he extends, but he delights in loving us and has more than enough strength for us in each new day.

How can you walk as one who knows God's faithfulness and understands his love for you?

GETTING BACK

As for you, return to your God,
hold fast to love and justice,
and wait continually for your God.

HOSEA 12:6 NRSV

Sometimes we lose our way and lose sight of the passion we once felt for God. Once we've lost our connection with him, we don't always know how to get back. We wonder if there is too much between us that he can't overlook.

But it's as simple as returning; as straightforward as getting down on your knees and saying, "God, I'm back." When you return, holding fast to the love that first drew you to him, God will show himself to you.

In which areas of life have you created distance between you and God? How can you change that?

Secrets of God

"Can you understand the secrets of God?
Can you search the limits of the Almighty?"

JOB 11:7 NCV

Have you ever discovered something about yourself that you never knew before? Maybe you tried a new food that you always claimed you hated, and you found you actually loved it. Maybe you were surprised by an idea you had that you didn't even know you were capable of.

If we, who are human, are so complex that we don't fully know ourselves, then how much more complex is the God who created us? We mustn't limit God to what we think we know of him. We cannot know his limits. But we can trust in his Word and his Holy Spirit to teach us as we seek to know him more.

What have you discovered about yourself recently?

The yes

The yes to all of God's promises is in Christ,
and through Christ we say yes to the glory of God.

2 CORINTHIANS 1:20 NCV

We all go through seasons in life when we doubt if God is really good to us. But tasting the goodness of God is often as simple as opening our hearts to receive what he has promised through Christ.

We may feel unworthy or even unready, but if we have said yes to salvation, then we have also said yes to God's promises, his goodness, and his eternal glory.

What promises of God can you say yes to today?

FILLING HUNGER

"I am the bread of life. Whoever comes to me will never be hungry,
and whoever believes in me will never be thirsty."

JOHN 6:35 NRSV

You don't have to teach babies to put things in their mouth—they are
born with a natural instinct to feed themselves. But you do need to teach
them *what* to feed themselves.

We were all created with a natural spiritual hunger for God. But we
must learn how to fill our hunger. There are things that we will try to
put into our souls that will never satisfy us. The only true remedy to
the deepest longing in our being is God—because we were created to
hunger after him.

How do you fill your hunger for God?

POWERFUL WORDS

"Son of man, let all my words sink deep into your own heart first.
Listen to them carefully for yourself."
EZEKIEL 3:10 NLT

There is so much power in quieting our minds and listening to the voice
of God as he speaks directly to us. We must learn to recognize his voice
above any other sound. God has the power and the ability to speak to
any situation we are going through, under any circumstance.

Since the beginning of time, God has begun powerful works with a
powerful Word. When we listen for him to speak, we ready ourselves for
him to do those works in and through us.

What powerful works do you want to do for God's kingdom?

Standing at the Last

Lord, you are my God;
I will exalt you and praise your name,
for in perfect faithfulness
you have done wonderful things.
things planned long ago.

ISAIAH 25:1 NIV

We serve a God who at the end, after everything has fallen and everything has changed, will still stand. In all of our confusion, suffering, and hopelessness, we have the enduring promise of serving the one who will always be greater.

It's easy to become discouraged in this life, but when we adjust our perspective to view everything against the backdrop of a victorious Savior, we can face absolutely anything with great confidence and peace.

What are you facing right now that requires confidence in a victorious God?

WATER AND BLOOD

This is He who came by water and blood—Jesus Christ; not only by water, but by water and blood. And it is the Spirit who bears witness, because the Spirit is truth.

1 JOHN 5:6 NKJV

Jesus didn't come to earth only to save us—he also came to heal us. He takes us as we are, but doesn't leave us that way. Jesus came with water to cleanse us from our sin and to heal us from the inside out.

He came with blood to sacrifice and to save us—trading his life for ours. Our salvation through Christ is complete as we are washed by the water and saved by the blood.

What do you want to ask the Lord to heal in you right now?

OUT OF DARKNESS

You are a chosen race, a royal priesthood, a holy nation, a people for God's own possession, so that you may proclaim the excellencies of Him who has called you out of darkness into His marvelous light.

1 PETER 2:9 NASB

Don't try to hide where you came from. No matter how dark or shameful your past was before you met Christ, there is power in your testimony. When a light is turned on in an already bright room, its effect is barely noticeable; but when even the smallest flicker of light appears in blackness, we are drawn to it.

We have been chosen as people of God's possession to proclaim his excellence and to be the visible evidence of his marvelous, life-changing light.

What is your testimony of being called out of darkness?

UNPUNISHED

He has not punished us as our sins should be punished;
he has not repaid us for the evil we have done.

PSALM 103:10 NCV

We deserve death, punishment, and distance from God because of our sin. But through the grace of salvation we have life, reward, and relationship with God. While the devil condemns us because of our sin and causes us to think that we have lost favor with God, the Holy Spirit convicts us of our sin and leads us to repentance and greater favor.

There isn't any condemnation for us in Christ Jesus because he died to remove our sin, our guilt, and our shame.

How do you remind yourself of your freedom from sin and guilt?

Live and Believe

"Everyone who lives and believes in me shall never die.
Do you believe this?"

JOHN 11:26 ESV

All throughout Scripture we are clearly promised eternal life through Christ. But there is something so poignant about the question in this verse: "Do you believe this?" Do you really, truly believe that you will live forever in heaven with Christ?

We are accustomed to promises being made and broken daily. Human fallacy has left us skeptical and anxious. But the beautiful truth is that we serve a God who will never back out of his covenant with us. Our hope of eternal life is sealed for us when we place our trust in Christ.

What do you believe about God's promises?

Accomplishment

Lord, you will grant us peace;
all we have accomplished is really from you.
ISAIAH 26:12 NLT

As we each look back on our lives, we remember what we've accomplished with some sense of pride. We have all climbed our mountains, but here we are—still standing to tell the tale.

As we reflect with peace in our hearts on things past, we must remember that we could have done none of it without God. He is the one who carries our burdens, comforts our hearts, strengthens our resolve, and orders our steps.

**What have you accomplished in your life
that you want to give God glory for?**

Unseen

We do not look at what we can see right now,
the troubles all around us, but we look forward to
the joys in heaven which we have not yet seen.
The troubles will soon be over, but the joys to come
will last forever.

2 CORINTHIANS 4:18 TLB

It's not easy to fix our eyes on something we can't see. By abandoning our earthly perspective in exchange for a heavenly one, we are radically changed. If we are focused only on what is here on earth, we will quickly find ourselves overwhelmed by fear and uncertainty.

If we fix our eyes on the promise of heaven, then we cannot help but be filled with peace, joy, and hope. We must remember that while we are here on earth for only a little while, it is the joy of heaven that will be our eternal, blessed reality.

**How can you fix your eyes on eternity rather than
on the momentary troubles around you?**

FAITHFUL

Let us hold fast the confession of our hope without wavering,
for he who promised is faithful.

HEBREWS 10:23 ESV

We don't have to question whether or not God will do what he said he would. He has proven himself to be faithful and true. When God makes us a promise, we don't have to wonder if he will follow through. It is we who are forgetful, fearful, and oftentimes, faithless.

Through the power of the Holy Spirit, the truth of the Word of God, and the encouragement of fellow believers, we can hold fast to the hope of our salvation, staying true to the confession we made when we first believed.

How do you make a habit of keeping your word?

MEASURED DAYS

LORD, let me know my end,
and what is the measure of my days;
let me know how fleeting my life is.
PSALM 39:4 NRSV

Life throws all kinds of things at us. Stress, pressure, decisions, and busy schedules. When we are living, rushed in the midst of our own lives, we forget the age-old reality that life passes very quickly. If we stop—as the Psalmist did—in full awareness of a fleeting life, we begin to recognize that what was once pressing is really trivial, and what was once urgent is actually insignificant.

By numbering our days and being mindful of our own fleeting existence on earth, we can spend our energies not on the pressures of earth, but rather on the purposes of heaven, which will last forever.

What are you pursuing right now that will last into eternity?

Not Shaken

Cast your burden upon the Lord and He will sustain you;
He will never allow the righteous to be shaken.

PSALM 55:22 NASB

We all have different ways of dealing with worry. Some internalize it, others call a friend, and still others find a way to take their minds off it. When we bring our worry to God and lay our anxious hearts bare before him, he will encourage us, lift us up, and sustain us. He will not allow us to be shaken or weakened by worry because he holds us through every situation.

The God who knows beginning from end is not flustered by our anxiety, and does not allow us to be overcome by uncertainty.

What anxiety do you need to give God today?

NEVER DISAPPOINTED

> This hope will never disappoint us, because God has poured out his love to fill our hearts. He gave us his love through the Holy Spirit, whom God has given to us.
>
> ROMANS 5:5 NCV

None of us are strangers to being disappointed. In life, we have learned to prepare ourselves for both the best and the worst possible outcomes. But when it comes to our salvation, there is no need to be braced for disappointment because the hope we have in Christ is guaranteed.

The presence of the Holy Spirit in our hearts reminds us constantly of this beautiful, certain promise we have in Christ.

How have you been disappointed lately?
Do you see God's hope in the situation?

REMEMBERING WONDERS

I will remember the deeds of the LORD;
yes, I will remember your wonders of old.

PSALM 77:11 ESV

When we find ourselves doubting God's power to work miracles in our lives, we must remember the wonders he has performed throughout history. Scripture is full of accounts of lives changed by the power of God.

The same great God who raised Lazarus from the dead is the God we worship today. The God who gave sight to a blind man and who let a lame man get up and walk still works miracles. Believe God for something great, knowing that his power has never lessened and his wonders never cease.

How can you grow in faith and expectation of God's greatness?

Because of the Poor

The Lord says,
"I will now rise up,
because the poor are being hurt.
Because of the moans of the helpless,
I will give them the help they want."

PSALM 12:5 NCV

God's economy is completely opposite from our own. Our currency is money and power, while his are mercy and grace. Our society elevates the rich and prominent, God lifts up the needy and nameless. His main objective isn't getting something from people; it's lavishing himself on them. His heart lies with the poor. He is a defender of the helpless and a protector of the weak.

If we desire to please the heart of the Father, then we too will take up the cause of the poor. We will defend them, rescue them, and help them. We will speak for them, honor them, and lavish love on them.

**What opportunities do you have to meet the needs of the poor
and to serve the helpless?**

FULLY DEVOTED

"Don't urge me to leave you or to turn back from you. Where you go I
will go, and where you stay I will stay. Your people will be my people
and your God my God."

RUTH 1:16 NIV

Ruth gave up everything she'd ever known to follow Naomi back
to Bethlehem—a land completely foreign to her. What a radical
commitment: to leave everything familiar for the sake of devotion to
another!

Are you willing to leave everything you love and know to follow God?
He is a God who rewards and repays. Everything you give up for the
kingdom will be restored to you in an even greater measure than you
gave up.

Where do you think God is leading you?

HUMAN EMPATHY

Rejoice with those who rejoice, weep with those who weep.
ROMANS 12:15 ESV

There are few things more remarkable than the power of human empathy. When someone is hurt, we can feel their pain although we are not wounded. When someone cries, we can weep with them although we are not sad. When someone laughs, we can enjoy the moment with them although the happiness is not our own.

Jesus came to us, as a human, in the greatest act of empathy in history. As we follow his example by shouldering each other's sorrows and by sharing in another's joy, we express his heart to the world.

How can you minister God's character to those around you?

MAKE A CHANGE

Do not conform to the pattern of this world, but be transformed by the renewing of your mind. Then you will be able to test and approve what God's will is—his good, pleasing and perfect will.

ROMANS 12:2 NIV

We want change, but we struggle to get or stay on task with our goals. "One day, I'll…" is the enemy of "Today, I am…"; yet it seems that as long as change hurts more than staying the same, we vacillate between our desires and our comfort.

It is often so with surrendering to the Holy Spirit. He longs to do "greater things than these," and while this appeals to us, the comfort of doing nothing seems reassuring, safe, and predictable. We find, at last, that the center of God's will truly is the safest place for our lives. Knowing that, we revel in him as he molds and inspires us. We were created to do good things.

What changes is God's Word making in your life?

Uniquely You

Just as each of us has one body with many members, and these members do not all have the same function, so in Christ we, though many, form one body, and each member belongs to all the others.

ROMANS 12:4-5 NIV

Each of us has a function. We don't operate like one another because we aren't fashioned that way. We often don't agree upon priorities—beyond dwelling in Christ and living in love—because we are each made to carry different aspects of God's glory.

So often, we read this verse as an adjuration to play nicely with people of other denominations. That's not it, though. It's a glorification of our wondrously creative God, and an encouragement to each take up our gifts, allowing others to do the same. Our gifts are just as personal as our salvation experiences. When we finally embrace our interdependence, we honor each other and operate in unity. We embrace who we are in Christ and let go of what we are not. To have the liberty to do so is an aspect of what it is to be truly free in Christ, and to operate in freedom.

What unique gifts do you have to offer others?

Leveling Up

Trust in the Lord with all your heart,
and do not lean on your own understanding.
In all your ways acknowledge him,
and he will make straight your paths.
PROVERBS 3:5-6 ESV

As we learn to walk in surrender to the Holy Spirit, our heavenly Father beckons us to a higher level of intimacy with him. In order to do this, we must become vulnerable and get real with him. We must continually trust him more than our experiences or reasoning.

When we trust God without boundaries, we find him more reliable than anyone else. We are wrapped in his love—the safest place we could find ourselves. Constantly leaning our hearts toward him, and choosing what he would, we receive his comfort and guidance, and our paths become straight.

What do you need to release control of?

RENEWED STRENGTH

I pray that the God who gives hope will fill you with much
joy and peace while you trust in him. Then your hope will overflow
by the power of the Holy Spirit.

ROMANS 15:13 NCV

Life takes a lot out of us. From sickness and pain to uncertainty
and sorrow, life's challenges can quickly drain us of our strength.
But for those who have put their hope in the Lord, there is a source
of refreshing.

For the one whose soul is tired and whose faith has all but dissolved,
there is renewal to be found in Jesus. When we turn to the promises
found in his Word and the joy found in his presence, we will be revived
by his Spirit—finding strength greater than our own.

How do you find strength in times of weariness?

FREEDOM

It is for freedom that Christ has set us free.
Stand firm, then, and do not let yourselves be burdened again
by a yoke of slavery.

GALATIANS 5:1 NIV

Christ paid a very high price for our freedom. With his life he purchased our salvation, and our emancipation from sin. When we choose to continue living in sin after our acceptance of Christ's work, it's as if a free man is willfully returning to bondage.

God's desire for us is that we live in complete freedom—freedom from sin, death, and the hopelessness of life without redemption. We must stand firm in the truth of our privilege, walking confidently in the freedom that was so dearly bought for us.

What steps can you take to live in freedom?

POWER TO TRANSFORM

We are made right with God by placing our faith in Jesus Christ.
And this is true for everyone who believes, no matter who we are.

ROMANS 3:22 NLT

God has the power to transform anything. We may think that a person or situation is completely beyond redemption—but God can reclaim even the most impossible of hearts and circumstances. We may have lost faith in believing for something, but God never does because he knows what he is capable of.

God, who has the power to speak the universe into existence, can certainly intervene in a situation and have his way in it. God, who commanded the dead to walk out of a tomb, can surely soften the heart of even the most hardened soul.

How can you trust God through the redemptive process?

Irony of Weakness

The Lord is the everlasting God,
the Creator of all the earth.
He never grows weak or weary.
No one can measure the depths of his understanding.
He gives power to the weak
and strength to the powerless.

ISAIAH 40:28-29 NLT

When you are stripped of your talents and strengths, you can do nothing but rely on the grace of God to carry you further. It is there, in your lacking, that God's power is truly revealed. None of us likes to feel inadequate, but if our inadequacy can further reveal Christ in us, it is always worth it.

We must remember that we are vessels of mercy—hallowed images of his grace that exist to always, first and foremost, bring glory to Christ.

How can you bring glory to God in your weakness today?

WEIGHT OF WORRY

Anxiety in a man's heart weighs him down,
but a good word makes him glad.

PROVERBS 12:25 ESV

Worry fills our head with questions that may never have answers and possibilities that may never come to pass. We become wearied as even our momentary troubles outweigh our peace. It is in these times that the encouraging words of a friend can become the catalyst to change our uncertainty into strength and our doubt into restored faith.

By surrounding ourselves with the type of people who regularly speak the truth, we unknowingly secure our own peace and future gladness.

Which friends in your life help relieve some of your anxiety? Why?

Joyful Remembrance

The LORD has done great things for us,
and we rejoiced.
PSALM 126:3 NRSV

We all have incredible stories to tell. These tapestries of our lives have been beautifully woven with a million moments of grace and wonder. Think back for a moment on some of the things God has done for you.

Your own remembrance of the miraculous amidst the ordinary will strengthen you as you rejoice in the great things he has done.

What miracles have been worked in your life?

GUIDED

I will lead the blind by a road they do not know,
by paths they have not known
I will guide them.
I will turn the darkness before them into light,
the rough places into level ground.
These are the things I will do,
and I will not forsake them.

ISAIAH 42:16 NRSV

When you feel that you have lost your way, and your feet can't feel the path beneath you, God promises that he will lead you forward. Even if you can't see what lies ahead, and though the road feels rocky and unsure, God will guide you. The path that seemed impassable will become smooth and the way that seemed impossible will become straightforward.

God promises that he will do this for you and more because he loves you and his is a love that never fails or forsakes.

**How can you trust God to guide you no matter
how impossible the way seems?**

SET APART

> "Sanctify them in the truth;
> Your word is truth."
>
> JOHN 17:17 NASB

We are bombarded with falsehood daily. Tabloids tout lies about public figures, newspapers print inaccuracies, television shows muddy reality, and social media is crowded with articles that haven't been properly fact checked. But in a world of misinformation, there is one source of truth that we can always trust—the Bible.

When we don't know where to look to find truth, we can always open his Word and be strengthened by the certainty of it. We are sanctified—set apart—by the truth found in Scripture.

What lies do you need to shine truth on today?

GOD OF SAFETY

Those who go to God Most High for safety
will be protected by the Almighty.
I will say to the LORD, "You are my place of safety and protection.
You are my God and I trust you."

PSALM 91:1-2 NCV

We all applaud the heroism of the young boy David when he took on the giant, Goliath. Or the boldness of Moses when he confronted Pharaoh about freeing the Israelites. But do we recognize that the same safety given to them has been given to us? They were regular people like us, who understood the power of the God they served.

Whatever you are facing right now, God is more than able to rescue you and keep you safe in the midst of it.

Who is your favorite hero of the faith and why?

Him Alone

The Lord your God you shall follow, him alone you shall fear,
his commandments you shall keep, his voice you shall obey,
him you shall serve, and to him you shall hold fast.

DEUTERONOMY 13:4 NRSV

God is gracious and kind, but he is also a jealous God. He wants to be enthroned by hearts given completely to him. There are many conflicting demands on our devotion: causes that impassion us, ideas that excite us, and visions that energize us. While our efforts for these things are just, they can often distract us from the one purpose that should hold our allegiance.

It is God we should follow with more zeal than anything else. We must be willing to let go of everything in order to serve him more fully.

How can you make God your one true passion?

Cleansed

Have mercy upon me, O God,
According to Your lovingkindness;
According to the multitude of Your tender mercies,
Blot out my transgressions.
Wash me thoroughly from my iniquity,
And cleanse me from my sin.

PSALM 51:1-2 NKJV

We should all long to be purified of our sin because it is in the cleansing from our iniquity that we are brought nearer to God. Our sin may be precious to us, but when we compare it to the treasure of closeness with the Father, it instantly loses its worth.

God doesn't harden his heart to a repentant believer. When we cry out to him in genuine remorse, he lavishes us with his mercy and love, washing us of our sin and restoring us to right relationship with him.

**Are there things you are genuinely remorseful about
that you want to offer to God today?**

WITHOUT FEAR

She is clothed with strength and dignity,
and she laughs without fear of the future.

PROVERBS 31:25 NLT

It's natural to fear the unknown. It can be frightening not to know what's coming or how to prepare for it. But you don't have to fear the future when you know whom you trust. You can live without anxiety about what is to come because you know that your life is in the hands of the one who controls it all.

When you are in Christ, you can smile at the mystery of the future with the peaceful and carefree heart of one who knows it is secure.

How do you submit your fears to God?

GREATER WONDER

When I look at your heavens, the work of your fingers,
the moon and the stars, which you have set in place,
what is man that you are mindful of him,
and the son of man that you care for him?

PSALM 8:3-4 ESV

The greatness of our God is displayed majestically throughout his creation. When we look into the night sky at all the twinkling stars and the far off planets, we realize almost instantly how small we are in his universe. But a greater wonder than the grandeur of God's capacity is his value for mankind.

The God of all this—the universe and everything in it—is the same God who gave his life to know us. The God who spoke the world into being is the same God who speaks quietly to our hearts. His love for us is as unsearchable as the heavens.

What part of God's creation are you most thankful for today?

Fully committed

"May your hearts be fully committed to the Lord our God,
to live by his decrees and obey his commands, as at this time."

1 KINGS 8:61 NIV

Is your heart fully committed to God? Or are other loves claiming your devotion? If your heart has truly been given to the Lord, then you will naturally follow his commands with your life. To be committed to someone is to be driven by a desire to please them—to give them your best because your own love demands it of you.

Regularly examine your heart to evaluate whether or not your full commitment lies with God, or if you are allowing your heart to become distracted by another love.

What other loves threaten your devotion to God?

TRUSTWORTHY

The word of the LORD holds true,
and we can trust everything he does.

PSALM 33:4 NLT

All of us have experienced our fair share of hurt. We've been jaded by failed dreams, broken relationships, and empty promises. No matter how hurt or worn down we may feel, we can always trust God with our hearts. He will never lie to us, manipulate us, or let us down. He will never go back on his word to us, abandon us, or stop loving us.

The Lord is always true to his Word. Who he has been throughout the ages is who he remains today. The God we read about in Scripture—who never forgot his covenants and loved irrevocably—is the same God who holds our hearts today.

Is broken trust hindering you from moving forward?

Go in peace

Then He said to the woman, "Your faith has saved you. Go in peace."

LUKE 7:50 NKJV

Each time after Jesus healed someone, he gave them the same command: "Go in peace." Jesus knew that even after the wonder of the miracle, there would be questions. Though outer healing had been given, inner turmoil would still threaten to overwhelm their hearts.

When Jesus heals someone, he heals them wholly. He doesn't just fix one problem, he saves the whole person. When we come to Christ, we are healed from the laws of sin and death and brought into a life of wholeness and peace. Our peace is a mark of our healing and we must walk confidently in it.

How can you claim healing and peace today?

Fascination

Those who love your teachings will find true peace,
and nothing will defeat them.
PSALM 119:165 NCV

The natural result of love is fascination: to be drawn to something so irresistibly that nothing can keep you from it. When we fascinate ourselves with the Word of God, we become an indestructible force in the spiritual realm.

We cannot be easily subjected to the lies of the enemy when our hearts have been saturated in the truth. By loving the teachings of God, his wisdom becomes our confidence and his presence our reward.

What most fascinates you about God?

Joyfully Waiting

I wait for the Lord, my whole being waits,
and in his word I put my hope.

PSALM 130:5 NIV

We so often think of waiting as hard, even unpleasant. But sometimes, waiting is wonderful: waiting to deliver great news, waiting for the birth of a child, the anticipation of giving a special gift.

When the thing we wait for is a good thing, waiting itself is a gift. This is how it is to wait for the Lord. With all our hope in him, the outcome is certain. The outcome is eternity. Let every part of us wait on him in joyful anticipation.

What are you waiting and hoping for today?

Though we stumble

The Lord makes firm the steps
of the one who delights in him;
though he may stumble, he will not fall,
for the Lord upholds him with his hand.

PSALM 37:23-24 NIV

Recall a near miss or two. The accident that almost happened, the plane you almost missed, the storm that began just a few seconds after you made it inside. Adrenaline pumping, we may forget to thank God for that extra boost of speed or the extra stopping power of our brakes.

Did we really almost fall, or were we given a glimpse of the Lord at work in our lives? As humans, we stumble; as his children, we are caught.

How have you seen the Lord's work in your life through near misses?

GOOD AND PERFECT

Whatever is good and perfect is a gift coming down to us from God our Father, who created all the lights in the heavens. He never changes or casts a shifting shadow.

JAMES 1:17 NLT

Take the next few minutes to pause and consider all the good, all the beauty in your life. You may be in a season that makes this easy, or perhaps now is a time that doesn't feel particularly "good and perfect."

Peonies in June, the wink of a quarter moon, loving and being loved, these are gifts from God. Your Father is a good father, a giver of good gifts. This doesn't change, even when your circumstances do.

What good and perfect gifts have you received from the Father lately?

Tears to Joy

Those who sow in tears
shall reap with shouts of joy!
PSALM 126:5 ESV

In times of sadness, whether from a fresh heartbreak or the memory of a distant one, it can seem like the pain will never end. No words of comfort, no matter how true or well-intentioned, can take away the ache.

These are the times we need only to crawl into our Abba's lap and allow his love and promises to envelop us in comfort. He won't say when, but he does assure us: we will shout again for joy.

What are you shedding tears about lately?
Can you let God comfort you?

NOT OF THE WORLD

"My prayer is not that you take them out of the world but that you protect them from the evil one. They are not of the world, even as I am not of it."

JOHN 17:15-16 NIV

When something is too wonderful to describe, we say it is out of this world. It is clearly from here, but something sets it apart as special.

It's the same way with us. We still go to our jobs, sleep in our beds, and do our best to love well and make a difference, but there is something different about those who belong to Jesus. We are no longer of this world. That makes us both special and vulnerable.

How do you see yourself as different than the world?

Under Protection

If you make the Lord your refuge,
if you make the Most High your shelter,
no evil will conquer you;
no plague will come near your home.
For he will order his angels to protect you wherever you go.

PSALM 91:9-11 NLT

Safety is big business. Consider all the product lines that exist to protect us: everything from sports equipment to security systems. For nearly every aspect of life, someone has a way to make you safer in it.

God knows our desire for security, and he offers protection like no amount of padding or technology could ever provide. He's got our eternal souls under his wing.

When do you feel most safe?

People of Light

Once you were full of darkness, but now you have light from the Lord.
So live as people of light! For this light within you produces only
what is good and right and true.

EPHESIANS 5:8-9 NLT

On an x-ray, a dark spot represents something that shouldn't be there. A tumor, a clot, a crack in the bone. For our bodies to function as they're meant to, these dark spots require attention and removal before they can harm us further.

Sin is a dark spot on our hearts. Jesus is the life-giving light that obliterates those dark places and makes us healthy and whole. He allows us to be people of light, reflecting his goodness and proclaiming his truth.

What dark spots do you want Jesus to wash clean today?

TRULY AWESOME

The heavens declare the glory of God;
the skies proclaim the work of his hands.
Day after day they pour forth speech;
night after night they reveal knowledge.

PSALM 19:1-2 NIV

Amazing beauty is all around us, so much so that we can become used to it. When was the last time you stopped to marvel at God's incredible creativity?

Study a flower. Read about the human eye. Watch the sun rise or set. Write down your dreams. Spend some time just soaking in the awesomeness of the Creator.

When did you last take time to marvel at God's creativity?

ALL OF YOU

"Love the Lord your God with all your heart and with all your soul and with all your mind and with all your strength."

MARK 12:30 NIV

Do you know how desperately the Father loves you? Replacing the myriad rules of the Old Testament, Jesus asks us to keep one beautiful commandment: love God with your entire being.

God wants to be loved with your heart, your soul, your mind, and your strength. Which of these do you find yourself most reluctant to give to him?

What can you give to God today?

ROCKS DON'T CHANGE

Trust in the LORD forever, for the LORD,
the LORD himself, is the Rock eternal.

ISAIAH 26:4 NIV

When people talk about the most dependable person they know, they may describe that person as being their rock. These people represent a constant in our lives; the advice they give today is the same advice they'll give in twenty years. Their principles—and their love—are unwavering.

A rock placed in a box for decades will look exactly the same on the day it's rediscovered. Rocks don't change.

What quality of God most reminds you of a rock?

Rest for your soul

"Take my yoke upon you and learn from me, for I am gentle and humble in heart, and you will find rest for your souls. For my yoke is easy and my burden is light."

MATTHEW 11:29-30 NIV

Choose a job: breaking up and moving rocks to prepare a field, or scattering seeds behind the plow. Back-breaking labor or a semi-leisurely stroll?

Jesus' invitation to walk with him is just such a choice. His way is love, trust, and dependence on the Father. Our way is, well, more like breaking up rocks. When he invites us to follow him, he invites us to lighten our loads.

What are you trying to bear alone?

NOTHING TO FEAR

In the multitude of my anxieties within me,
Your comforts delight my soul.
PSALM 94:19 NKJV

Worry. Stress. Anxiety. Chances are, just reading those words heightened your own levels of each. Fear is one of the greatest threats to the peace we have in the Lord.

As we become consumed by the many pressures of this world, it's easy to take our eyes off the comforter of our soul: God's Holy Spirit. Just as easily, let us turn back to him and watch our many worries fade into insignificance.

How does God's comfort ease your worries?

Completely Attuned

When I said, "My foot is slipping,"
your unfailing love, LORD, supported me.
PSALM 94:18 NIV

A good surgical assistant knows what instrument the surgeon needs before they ask for it. A mother can spot a stuffy nose or broken heart the minute her child enters the room; the right words and a hug are waiting. Attentiveness: it's part of the job.

The Lord is completely attuned to your needs. Long before you fall, his arm waits to steady you. He's right here with you, always.

How has God's attentiveness blessed you recently?

Peace With God

Since we have been justified through faith,
we have peace with God through our Lord Jesus Christ.
ROMANS 5:1 NIV

Do you ever wonder if you please God? Sometimes this question rolls around in a believer's mind, subconsciously or consciously. For a child of God, it's a rather easy answer. We need to train our hearts and minds with the answer so we don't needlessly torment ourselves.

There is one way alone to peace with God. If you have received Christ as your Lord, then the faith it took you to believe that justified you before God. Your faith in Christ makes you no longer guilty. Because of that, you can have peace. Dear child, don't wonder. God is not like us—fickle and hard to please. He is pleased with his Son's sacrifice and your faith in it.

How can you remain in God's peace?

Fulfill His Purpose

The LORD will fulfill his purpose for me;
your steadfast love, O LORD, endures forever.
Do not forsake the works of your hands.

PSALM 138:8 ESV

Did you know God is more intent on fulfilling his purpose for your life than you are? He is fully aware you are the weaker vessel in your relationship with him. While we might have zeal and passion, we naturally grow weak, lazy, or idle. This can be discouraging to us, but God is not easily discouraged. After all, he is our Maker and knows exactly how frail we are.

God can fulfill his purpose for you because his love will endure over you forever. It is not a weak love. You are the precious work of his hands.

**How can you trust and partner with God in fulfilling
his purpose for your life?**

Pilgrimage with God

Blessed are those whose strength is in you,
whose hearts are set on pilgrimage.
They go from strength to strength,
till each appears before God in Zion.

PSALM 84: 5-7 NIV

The Psalmist gives us a picture of what it is like to be on a pilgrimage with God. Every Christian begins their journey as a pilgrim, and it doesn't end until we are with him forever. Anyone who has walked even a little way on this journey knows the pilgrimage is not always—or ever—a smoothly paved path. There are mountaintops and valleys.

Another name for Valley of Baca is Valley of Weeping. Just because we are headed to Zion does not mean we won't struggle. For the believers who continue, they will see that they aren't getting weaker but stronger. This is because the longer they walk, the more they learn their strength isn't in themselves.

How do you feel spiritually stronger today than you did last year?

Rooted in Love

You, O Lord, are a God merciful and gracious,
slow to anger and abounding in steadfast love and faithfulness.
PSALM 86:15 NRSV

It is so important, as God's children, that we are confident in his character. In Ephesians 3:17, Paul prays that we be rooted and established in God's love. This means our roots are buried deep in the soil of his love, and we drink all our sustenance through those roots.

As you remain confident of his love, you can receive correction and direction from him without offense because you know it comes from a heart of love.

How do you remain confident in God's love for you?

UNCONDITIONAL ACCEPTANCE

Accept one another, then, just as Christ accepted you,
in order to bring praise to God.
ROMANS 15:7 NIV

If she gossiped less. If he shared his feelings more. It's easy, isn't it, to list the ways other people could change for the better? We know we are called to live in harmony with one another, but our "others" can really make it difficult.

But we need to accept one another as Christ accepted us. Jesus takes us as we are: broken, imperfect, sinful. If this is how the Savior welcomes us, who are we to put conditions on our acceptance of anyone else?

How can you show others unconditional acceptance?

READY TO SEE

Open my eyes that I may see
wonderful things in your law.
PSALM 119:18 NIV

Think back to a time you suddenly understood something. Maybe you were late to get the punchline of a joke, or maybe you finally understood why your mom wouldn't let you wear something to school. "Oh…I get it!" you said.

The Bible is filled with "Aha" moments. As we go deeper into the Word, God opens our eyes to things we never noticed before. Stories we've heard all our lives become fresh with new insights. Truths we've taken for granted take on new weight and significance as we discover the Word is alive.

What beauty and depth have you found hidden in God's Word?

Heart That Cares

God is working in you, giving you the desire and the power
to do what pleases him.

PHILIPPIANS 2:13 NLT

What was your last random act of kindness? Whether you bought a homeless man a burger, donated to dig a new well in Africa, or simply smiled at a stranger in the produce aisle, these impulses are evidence of the Spirit at work in your life.

The more we tune into God, the more he will work in us. As we focus our thoughts on his perfect love and look to him for inspiration, he provides us with opportunities—big and small—to express his love to others.

How can you share God's love and goodness with someone today?

TWIG BY TWIG

The wise woman builds her house,
But the foolish pulls it down with her hands.
PROVERBS 14:1 NKJV

If you were to see a mother bird ripping her nest apart, how would you react? It's hard to imagine, isn't it? Now consider a woman you know who is too busy to attend a soccer game, return a phone call, or write a sympathy card. Sadly, it's not so hard to imagine. Maybe you even saw yourself.

Choice by choice, twig by twig, we have the option to build our homes, our lives, our relationships, or destroy them. When we keep our attention on the Father, he gives us the strength to keep building.

**What steps can you take to reinforce your connectedness
with the people you love?**

JUST BECAUSE

Honor the LORD for the glory of his name.
Worship the LORD in the splendor of his holiness.
PSALM 29:2 NLT

It isn't your birthday, but there's a gift on the counter with your name on it. You haven't done anything particularly special lately, but a card arrives in the mail to let you know you are loved—just because. It feels wonderful. It feels even better when you are on the giving end.

When is the last time you worshipped God just for being God? He loves to receive spontaneous gifts of love, honor, and praise just as much as we do.

How can you honor the Lord today?

SiGHT UNSEEN

Though you have not seen him, you love him; and even though
you do not see him now, you believe in him and are filled with an
inexpressible and glorious joy.

1 PETER 1:8 NIV

How did you first fall in love with Jesus? Unlike human love, one of the
great mysteries of faith is how we can know so surely and love so deeply
he whom we've never actually seen. But we can. We do.

One of the great rewards of faith is the "inexpressible and glorious joy"
the Holy Spirit places in our hearts the moment we believe. Have you
claimed your joy today?

Write down how you know that God is real.

Cookie Jar Prayers

If my people, who are called by my name, will humble themselves and pray and seek my face and turn from their wicked ways, then I will hear from heaven, and I will forgive their sin and will heal their land.

2 CHRONICLES 7:14 NIV

Even young children understand cause and effect. "If I am naughty, I get a time out. If I say please, I get a cookie." Often, we approach prayer with the same way. "If I pray, he listens." But does he?

We must humbly seek his face and turn from our sins so we can be forgiven and heard.

What have you been praying about lately?

He Never Sleeps

He will not let you stumble;
the one who watches over you will not slumber.

PSALM 121:3 NLT

How long can you go without sleep? Most of us have gone all night at least once, but we also collapsed, exhausted, as soon as we were able. No matter how important the task, how critical the vigil, we all have to take a break eventually.

All except God. The one who watches over you, the one who makes sure you won't stumble as you climb today's mountain, never stops watching. Always and forever, night and day, he's got you.

**How does it make you feel to think
that God never stops watching over you?**

No Darkness

This is the message we have heard from him and declare to you:
God is light; in him there is no darkness at all.

1 JOHN 1:5 NIV

In total darkness, we instinctively seek light. We turn on our phones, fumble for a light switch, light a candle. With a single light source, the darkness can be overcome. We can find our way.

This same principle applies to our hearts. God is pure light, and with him, we can overcome any darkness we face. No temptation, no addiction, no sin is too powerful for God to conquer.

How can you shine light on the darkness you are battling right now?

HE CHOSE YOU

The LORD is all I need.
He takes care of me.
My share in life has been pleasant;
my part has been beautiful.

PSALM 16:5-6 NCV

If you are a follower of Christ, God chose precisely when and how to invite you to join his family. You received the most prestigious, coveted invitation in history. He chose you.

Maybe you simply yearned for more meaning in your life and he led you into a Christian community. Perhaps you needed a radical life change, to shed an addiction or other destructive pattern, and you felt him lift you out of the darkness. Regardless of how it happened, he called you by name, and now you are his.

How do you feel chosen by God?

HiDDEN TREASURE

He opened their minds so they could understand the Scriptures.
LUKE 24:45 NIV

It's amazing, isn't it, to watch a movie or read a book you remember from childhood and see all you missed back then? Like uncovering hidden treasure, our adult minds understand bits of humor, layers of context and subtext in a way we couldn't as children.

When it comes to our faith and our understanding of the Scriptures, we are all as children. God chooses what to show us and when, so like that favorite childhood story or film, the Bible can feel brand new every time we return to it.

What treasures have you found in God's Word lately?

MORE OF YOU

"He must become greater; I must become less."

JOHN 3:30 NIV

Imagine you're famous. People follow you, listen to you, and genuinely respect you. Now, imagine willingly, even happily giving it all up. How did that feel? For most of us, sacrificing that fame wasn't easy—and it wasn't even real. Humility is hard. It's also a requirement for a Christ-centered life.

John the Baptist, one of the most truly humble people in all of Scripture, spoke the words of John 3:30. He knew it was time for Jesus to fulfill the prophecies, which meant it was time for him to point others toward Jesus—and away from himself.

What agenda and desires do you need to set aside for God right now?

INCOMPREHENSIBLE GIFT

When people work, their wages are not a gift, but something they have earned. But people are counted as righteous, not because of their work, but because of their faith in God who forgives sinners.

ROMANS 4:4-5 NLT

No matter how much a person loved their job, if their employer stopped paying them, they'd eventually stop working. Conversely, if the employee stopped working, the employer would inevitably stop signing paychecks. In an employment agreement, both parties have to honor their part for it to work.

This is what makes our relationship—our mutual agreement—with Jesus so astonishing. His part of the agreement was death on a cross to ensure our salvation. Our part is belief.

How is God's gift of salvation something you cannot earn?

WHERE ARE YOU

Then the Lᴏʀᴅ God called to the man, "Where are you?"
GENESIS 3:9 NLT

When adults play hide-and-seek with children, they usually know exactly where the kids are hiding. Still, they play along for the benefit of the little ones. "Where could she be?" they playfully wonder aloud. The period of life when we believe we can hide in plain sight is brief, and full of discovery.

When Adam and Eve first sinned, God took on a similar role. He knew exactly where they were (and what they'd done), yet he called to them, "Where are you?" In order for them to begin the healing process, they first had to realize—and confess—where they were.

What are you trying to hide from God today?

HELD

"I, the LORD your God,
hold your right hand;
it is I who say to you, 'Fear not,
I am the one who helps you.'"

ISAIAH 41:13 ESV

Looking back on the hardest, scariest things we've ever done, we often wonder where we found the courage. How on earth did we face that diagnosis, pass that exam, give that eulogy?

Scripture assures us our help comes from heaven, from God himself. He is the inner voice saying, "You can get through this. You are strong enough." That sudden burst of strength, bravery, or initiative? That was the Lord, squeezing your hand.

When do you sense the Lord helping you?

Not for nothing

I do not set aside the grace of God, for if righteousness could be gained through the law, Christ died for nothing!

GALATIANS 2:21 NIV

For weeks, you've prepared. Extra study sessions, flash cards, copious notes. Finally, you're ready. You enter the classroom and see this message: "Test canceled. Everyone gets an A." All that work. All for nothing.

If we believe we can get to heaven by working hard, we're saying Jesus' brutal death was for nothing. Until we accept his gift of grace, we're toiling—needlessly—and worse, we're relegating Jesus' ultimate sacrifice to a mere gesture.

How can you let go of trying to earn a place in heaven?

YOU ARE CHOSEN

God decided in advance to adopt us into his own family by bringing us to himself through Jesus Christ. This is what he wanted to do, and it gave him great pleasure.

EPHESIANS 1:5 NLT

Adopted children never have to wonder if they were wanted. They grow up with the certainty that their parents chose them. What a blessing.

As a child of God, you are granted that same wonderful knowledge. You are his adopted one, chosen specially to bring him pleasure. Not to accomplish any great feat, or to fulfill any grand purpose, but just because he wanted you.

How do you feel when you consider you have been adopted into God's family?

SHELTERED

He will cover you with his feathers.
He will shelter you with his wings.
His faithful promises are your armor and protection.

PSALM 91:4 NLT

Like an eagle, God shelters us beneath his wings from storms and attacks. The image is powerful, yet also tender. How wonderful it is to be tucked in, right up against him, absorbing his warmth!

Do you rest in this promise of protection, or do you struggle, always poking your head out to see what dangers await? Maybe you've even tried to leave the nest altogether and take care of yourself. If so, return to his side. Accept his protection.

What do you need shelter from today?

Carry the Shield

In all circumstances take up the shield of faith,
with which you can extinguish all the flaming darts of the evil one.
EPHESIANS 6:16 ESV

To lose someone in an accident is devastating. To learn it could have been prevented adds immeasurably to the pain. "A seatbelt could have saved her," are heavy words to carry.

As part of the armor of God, the shield of faith allows us to quench flaming arrows—but only if we hold it up. It's our responsibility to hold onto our faith and carry it wherever we go. Setting it down, even briefly, leaves us vulnerable to attack.

What armor do you need to put on today?

JUST SAY NO

Submit yourselves, then, to God. Resist the devil,
and he will flee from you.

JAMES 4:7 NIV

Submit to God; resist the devil. It seems simple, so why do culture—and our own lives—so often say the opposite? How often do we give in to temptation and resist the one leading us to our best life?

Until we surrender our lives to the one who wants only good for us, only peace and light, we are subject to the one who wants to destroy us. He will leave, running scared, but not until we stand with God and tell him "no."

How can you submit your life to God again today?

LIVE AT PEACE

If it is possible, as far as it depends on you, live at peace with everyone.

ROMANS 12:18 NIV

How does this verse strike you? One extreme, you may think, "Ha! He doesn't know the people in my life." On the other hand, this may be one of the easiest commands in Scripture. You're just that easy-going.

Most of us lie somewhere in the middle. We get along with almost everyone—there's just that one co-worker. And that temperamental middle child. And... live at peace with everyone? We can't control other people, but with Christ's help, we can control our response to them.

Which responses do you need to better control through Christ?

PEACE AND QUIET

The work of righteousness will be peace,
And the effect of righteousness, quietness and assurance forever.

ISAIAH 32:17 NKJV

Peace and quiet. Just saying those words together can bring comfort. It can also bring despair, if they seem out of reach. How, oh how can we claim them?

Through righteousness comes peace, quietness, and assurance. Forever. It's a big word, righteousness, and one you may have shied away from. If so, lean in. Righteousness is not an unattainable ideal of perfection or superiority. It's about putting God first, and living in a way that honors him. In exchange for your honor, he offers the peace and quiet you long for.

What does living a righteous life look like to you?

Questions

As you do not know the path of the wind,
or how the body is formed in a mother's womb,
so you cannot understand the work of God,
the Maker of all things.

ECCLESIASTES 11:5 NIV

"Why?" Call to mind a toddler who has just grasped the meaning and power of this wonderful little word. Over and over, to everything they hear, they respond, "Why?"

As we grow we learn to stop asking why so often, but inside our minds, we maintain a powerful desire to know. It is human nature. However, when it comes to the mind of God, we cannot satisfy this desire. His mind—his ways—cannot be known. Accepting and even embracing this truth is a sign of spiritual growth.

What questions are you asking God today? Can you see his sovereignty?

Coffee With God

I rise before dawn and cry for help;
I wait for Your words.
PSALM 119:147 NASB

How is the morning for you? Do you rise before you need to, eager to start your day, or is the snooze button your best friend? If you are in the former group, do you begin your day with God?

Numerous times in Scripture, we are encouraged to be morning people. For some, this advice is not even necessary; for others, it seems impossibly out of reach. "I'm just not wired that way," we say. Perhaps, if this is us, a rewiring is in order. If you knew you had a coffee date with the Father, would you even need an alarm?

How can you ensure you spend time with God each day?

Spirited Worship

"God is Spirit, so those who worship him must worship
in spirit and in truth."

JOHN 4:24 NLT

How do you define "spirit"? A feisty, hard to break horse is considered spirited. An athlete overcoming great hardship is said to have an indomitable spirit. In both examples, what's being described is something beyond the body. And so it is with the Spirit of God.

We may think we know him the least, but consider this: God the Father and Jesus the Son are in heaven. It is the Holy Spirit intervening in our lives, teaching, comforting, and protecting us. It is the Spirit who is our intimate companion, and he is wholly deserving of our worship.

How do you feel God influencing and guiding the course of your life?

REAL LOVE

Since ancient times no one has heard,
no ear has perceived,
no eye has seen any God besides you,
who acts on behalf of those who wait for him.

ISAIAH 64:4 NIV

Authenticity. It matters, doesn't it? We wonder if the gem, the handbag, the promise, is real. We've all heard the expression, "If it's too good to be true, it's probably not," so we scrutinize the people and possessions in our lives, looking for authenticity.

What great comfort we can take in our God: the one, true God! All his promises are true; all his gifts are good. His love is authentic, and it is ours to claim.

How can you be authentic in your love for God?

FOOLISH ONES

"The eyes of the LORD search the whole earth in order to strengthen those whose hearts are fully committed to him. What a fool you have been! From now on you will be at war."

2 CHRONICLES 16:9 NLT

You blew it. Those three words carry a weight none of us wishes to bear, yet at some point we all must. That actions have consequences is a hard, painful truth. Perhaps you are living it now.

Be encouraged. Yes, you will face many trials, but because of Jesus' work on the cross, you need never face them alone.

Where do you seek approval and satisfaction?

TELL THE STORY

Let the redeemed of the Lord tell their story—
those he redeemed from the hand of the foe.

PSALM 107:2 NIV

What's your story? Whether it's so complex you barely know where to begin, or you think it's too insignificant to tell, be assured that it matters.

From the beginning, God had you in mind. He planned you out to the tiniest detail. He has loved you forever. The way in which you discovered this beautiful truth, or the way it is currently unfolding, is of great significance. Begin telling it to yourself, and be ready to share it when the time comes.

What is your story?

SELF-IMPORTANCE

Humble yourselves under the mighty power of God,
and at the right time he will lift you up in honor.
1 PETER 5:6 NLT

Traffic jams. Grocery store lines on Saturday mornings. The DMV. Did your heart just quicken? Unless you have a great book to read—or you were born with the proverbial "patience of a saint,"—waiting is, at best, an inconvenience.

Have you ever stopped to wonder why? Pondering patience leads to exploring another uncomfortable concept: humility. We're impatient, but why? Is our time any more important than anyone else's? To God, the answer is an unequivocal "no."

How can you become more patient?

Written in Stone

God's truth stands firm like a foundation stone with this inscription:
"The Lord knows those who are his," and "All who belong to the Lord
must turn away from evil."

2 TIMOTHY 2:19 NLT

Among friends, rules evolve. There are flexible policies: "Monday night is Girls Night," and there are unbreakable codes of friendship: "If you wouldn't say it to her face, don't say it." That rule, we say, is written in stone.

In his second letter to Timothy, Paul shares an important truth in two parts: First, the Lord knows you as his own. Second, those who are his must turn from sin. This matters, we learn, enough to be written in stone.

How do you successfully turn from sin?

SURRENDER

"Be strong, and let us be courageous for our people and for the cities of our God; and may the LORD do what seems good to him."

1 CHRONICLES 19:13 NRSV

How often do you struggle with God for control of your life, asking for certain outcomes, wanting things to go your way? Is surrender to his plan easy for you or a constant challenge?

In the words of Joab to his army, we find a perfect example of the surrendered life: be strong for those we serve; be courageous for the Kingdom of God, and may the Lord's will be done. Nothing for himself, all for the Master. Oh, that we could achieve such trust and devotion!

What do you need to let God control today?

FOOL FOR YOU

The message of the cross is foolishness to those who are perishing,
but to us who are being saved it is the power of God.

1 CORINTHIANS 1:18 NIV

We may have fallen for a few pranks in our lives or been at the receiving
end of someone's joke. We have all had times where our faith has been
ridiculed. In these times, it is good to be reminded that human wisdom is
nothing in comparison to God's wisdom.

True wisdom is believing in Jesus Christ and accepting his salvation
for your life. This can seem like foolishness to the world, but to you it is
access to the power of God. You are wise to have chosen to be a fool for
Jesus!

How do you explain your faith?

I AM FOUND

"Rejoice with me; I have found my lost sheep."

LUKE 15:6 NIV

How pleasing it is to find something that we thought we had lost! We rejoice in the small victories of finding a lost receipt, pair of sunglasses, or even that matching sock! There is something in our created nature that tells us loss is something to be grieved and discovery is to be celebrated!

The parable of the lost sheep makes it abundantly clear that Jesus celebrates every life that is found in him. The heavens celebrate your salvation, and though you are one of many, Jesus has gone out of the way to find you. Such is his love for his own.

How can you be confident in your significance to God?

BLOTTED OUT

"I, even I, am He who blots out your transgressions for My own sake;
And I will not remember your sins."

ISAIAH 43:25 NKJV

We are not unlike the Israelites, turning from God's ways time and time again. Yet God was merciful to his beloved people; his love was enough to forget their sins. He didn't just cover them up, he completely removed them.

How incredible to know that God removes our sins and remembers them no more. You have been forgiven, and will continue to be forgiven, because in his love, God will always show you mercy. Let your heart be free from condemnation and walk assuredly in his grace.

How can you forget about your sin?

CITIZENS OF HEAVEN

Our citizenship is in heaven, from which we also eagerly wait for the Savior, the Lord Jesus Christ.

PHILIPPIANS 3:20 NKJV

How great it is to be reminded of home when we are far from it. Sometimes a familiar voice, smell, or picture is enough to trigger a longing to return to where we belong. Paul reminds believers that we belong in heaven, a place that we were truly made for.

Eternity is in our hearts because we were made for the same glory as Jesus! Heaven is our home. Sometimes we don't long for heaven because we are too focused on our earthly home. We can remind ourselves today that we are citizens of heaven and someday we will be where we truly belong.

What about eternity excites you the most?

HEART OF COMPASSION

Jesus, when He came out, saw a great multitude and was moved
with compassion for them, because they were like sheep not having
a shepherd.

MARK 6:34 NKJV

When Jesus saw the crowds, he didn't just see them as a bothersome
multitude, he saw them as people with needs. Like sheep without a
shepherd, people are lost and they need our help. Sometimes the needs
are obvious—like help with a newborn or food for the hungry. Other
needs are deeper, like the need to have a friend or be healed from
emotional pain.

Jesus has compassion! Because we know this loving Jesus, we can have
compassion for others. He is able to provide for your needs and he will
give you the strength to help others.

How can you show compassion to others today?

SING

Sing praises to God, sing praises!
Sing praises to our King, sing praises!
For God is the King of all the earth;
Sing praises with understanding.

PSALM 47:6-7 NKJV

We may not all have the voice of an angel, but we can all sing, no matter how good or bad it sounds to us. God created you with a voice and with lips that can praise him for all the good things he has done. He is the king of the earth and the king of our hearts. He will delight in your song of praise, even if he is the only one that appreciates it!

So, sing praises to God. Sing, because you understand his goodness. Sing, because you understand his grace. Sing, because he is worthy!

What are some of your favorite worship lyrics?

POWERFUL PROMISES

He did not waver through unbelief regarding the promise of God,
but was strengthened in his faith and gave glory to God, being fully
persuaded that God had power to do what he had promised.

ROMANS 4:20-21 NIV

Abraham and Sarah were aged when they were told that God would
give them a child. They had good reason not to believe this as it seemed
absurd in the natural sense. Sarah even laughed! Yet Abraham let his
belief rest in the power of God.

We serve a God who is more than able to carry out his promises!
Abraham was given as an example because he looked beyond the
circumstance to the greatness of God. When you have a revelation of
the power of God, your faith will be strengthened and you will have
confidence in God's promises to you, and to this world.

How has God revealed his greatness to you?

Everlasting Beauty

Charm is deceitful and beauty is passing,
But a woman who fears the Lord, she shall be praised.

PROVERBS 31:30 NKJV

At some point in our lives we are either going to struggle with jealously of those who are better looking than ourselves, or the fact that our outward beauty is passing. The fact is beauty can consume much of our time.

The Bible, however, honors those with a heart for God. Remember this when you are lamenting your outward appearance. You are praised because your heart toward God and your service to him is beautiful. His grace has produced a beauty in you that will never fade.

What is beauty to you?

RESTORED

The LORD opens the eyes of the blind;
The LORD raises up those who are bowed down;
The LORD loves the righteous.

PSALM 146:8 NASB

Our God loves to restore life to his creation. When Jesus came to earth, he healed many physical needs. Greater than physical healing, Jesus came to restore our spiritual brokenness. He opened eyes to the truth, ministered to the poor in spirit, and restored believers to righteousness.

How blessed you are. He has opened your eyes, he will always lift you up in times of trouble, and he loves you because you have chosen the path of righteousness. Let the God of encouragement and restoration be your strength today.

What needs to be restored in your life today?

Be teachable

Instruct the wise and they will be wiser still;
teach the righteous and they will add to their learning.

PROVERBS 9:9 NIV

The writer of these words knew that a wise person is not just one who has a lot of knowledge. The wise listen to instruction; they continue to seek out wise ways. In the same way, the righteous want to add to the truth they already know.

Is your heart open to receive instruction? Do you want to add to your knowledge of the truth of God's Word? God delights in your pursuit of him and he will instruct and teach you to be wiser still!

When has your heart been willing to receive God's instruction most?

Peace seeds

The seed whose fruit is righteousness is sown in peace
by those who make peace.

JAMES 3:18 NASB

Peaceful ways give birth to righteousness. There are times when conflict cannot be avoided, but assuming the role of the peacemaker is often far better than getting your own way. To be a peacemaker requires humility and the desire for the greater good.

One of the many names of Jesus is the Prince of Peace. He is our best example of what it means to sow peace and to make peace. He lives in you, and by drawing on him, you will experience peace in times of trouble and conflict.

How can you become a peacemaker so the fruit you bear in your life will be that of righteousness?

Very good creation

God saw everything that He had made, and indeed it was very good.
GENESIS 1:31 NKJV

On the sixth day, after all other created things, God made man and woman. He made us in his image. On that day he declared that his creation was very good. How reassuring it is to know that God's creation was intentionally good. He did not create mistakes or flaws; he created us according to his perfect plan.

The next time you find yourself despairing about all the things that have gone wrong in this world, go back to the beginning. He created all things good. Yes, sin has taken us a long way from this goodness, but God's plan isn't finished yet; he is coming to restore his creation and it will once again be very good!

What do you find very good about God's creation?

No more pain

He will wipe away every tear from their eyes,
and death shall be no more,
neither shall there be mourning, nor crying, nor pain anymore,
for the former things have passed away.

REVELATION 21:4 ESV

We are promised a time when there will be no more pain. This life is full of hardship, but we can live in hope that a day will come where joy will reign supreme!

It is this hope that carries us through the hard times, when we trust that God is still good and that he has good plans for us now and in the future. Rejoice in eternal life, for this is not where it ends!

What physical, emotional, or spiritual needs are most pressing in your life right now?

BRAVE HEART

> "Have I not commanded you? Be strong and courageous!
> Do not tremble or be dismayed, for the LORD your God is with you
> wherever you go."
>
> JOSHUA 1:9 NASB

Joshua had a big task ahead of him: to lead the entire nation of Israel into the Promised Land. This required defeating great opposition. God reassured Joshua many times with these words, "Be strong and courageous." When God calls his people to do his will, he empowers them with the ability to do it.

You are called of God and are able to do his work because he is with you wherever you go. You are not expected to walk in your own strength. This is why God instructs us to have courage. Our God is a mighty God and we can do all things through him.

What do you need courage for today?

MERE MORTALS

In God, whose word I praise—
in God I trust and am not afraid.
What can mere mortals do to me?

PSALM 56:4 NIV

"In God We Trust." This is still printed on US currency despite many people not truly trusting or believing in God. As Christians, we claim to trust God too. Is this a motto that is written on the currency of your heart—one that you can hold fast to in times when all else seems against you?

We are not always spared harm or hurt, but God is always present and promises to take care of us. It is important to remember that no matter what we face, no "mere mortal" can ever take away our eternal destiny in Jesus.

How do you place your trust fully in God?

Practice peace

Keep on doing the things that you have learned and received and
heard and seen in me, and the God of peace will be with you.
PHILIPPIANS 4:9 NRSV

Paul was chosen by God to carry the good news of Jesus Christ to all
who were willing to receive it. His messages to the believers guided them
in the truth about Jesus and how to live a righteous life.

We have been blessed to have all of this truth available to us through the
Bible. But we need to be more than just good readers or listeners. We are
encouraged to keep practicing the things that we have learned through
God's Word. When we put the truth into action, we are rewarded with
the knowledge of the presence of God near to us.

How can you practice peace today?

Church Siblings

He has given us this command:
Anyone who loves God must also love their brother and sister.

1 JOHN 4:21 NIV

Family members can be some of the hardest people to get along with! In the same way, people within our church or community of believers are not always easy to show love to.

We cannot separate our love for God from our love for others. When we love God, we obey his commands and he desires that we have right relationships with each other. Be encouraged that you have been given a family of brothers and sisters in Christ, and they are there to love you as you choose to love them.

How can you show love to your community of believers?

STARRY HOST

You alone are the LORD. You made the heavens, even the highest
heavens, and all their starry host, the earth and all that is on it, the seas
and all that is in them. You give life to everything, and the multitudes
of heaven worship you.

NEHEMIAH 9:6 NIV

It is amazing enough that the Lord made the earth and everything in it,
from the blade of grass to the complexities of conception. Even more
amazing is that he created the heavens, the universe, and everything
beyond it. There are created things that we will not get to see or
understand while we are limited by our earthly bodies and knowledge.

God gave life to everything that he created. It is not only on earth that we
worship God. He is worshipped in all creation. What an amazing God we
serve; he is worthy of our praise.

How is God shown through creation?

ON YOUR BEHALF

He is able to save completely those who come to God through him,
because he always lives to intercede for them.

HEBREWS 7:25 NIV

When Jesus died on the cross and rose again, he not only took the
penalty for our sin, he also became the way in which we can approach
God boldly. He made us holy.

It is only through Jesus that we are saved, and the Bible said that he is
always interceding for us—past, present, and future. How encouraging to
know that we have someone who stands on our behalf to declare us holy
and righteous.

What do you want Jesus to intercede for in your life?

DEBT OF LOVE

Let no debt remain outstanding, except the continuing debt to love one another, for whoever loves others has fulfilled the law.

ROMANS 13:8 NIV

When a bill arrives in the mail, we are reminded that we owe money in return for something that has been done for us. If we leave it for too long, it can cause anxiety and even resentment on both sides. This is one reason the Scripture reminds us not to leave a debt outstanding.

However, the Bible instructs us to treat love as debt, in the sense that we should continually be compelled to love one another and to give love even if it has not been earned! This is the extreme love that God has shown us. Let his unending and unconditional love for you be the reminder letter that you need to spur you on to love others in the same way.

In what ways does Jesus' love still amaze you?

His Riches

This same God who takes care of me will supply all your needs from his glorious riches, which have been given to us in Christ Jesus.

PHILIPPIANS 4:19 NLT

The Lord's riches are found in his goodness, his grace, and his sovereignty as king over all. God is always able to provide for all of our needs. Sometimes we may feel as though we are not worthy to receive from the Lord. Sometimes we find it hard to trust and we worry about our needs.

The good news of Jesus Christ is that he has given us access to the throne of God. You are a child of the king and he offers his riches to you. All you need to do is love him, ask him, and trust in his goodness. His promise is to take care of you.

What do you need right now? Can you trust God to provide for you?

WATER WAYS

Let justice flow like a river,
and let goodness flow like a never-ending stream.

AMOS 5:24 NCV

We all have a sense of needing to keep things fair, that's why we have referees at sports matches, lines at the store, and a judge at a court case. When we see or experience injustice, we long for it to be made right.

We know that God is just and that he also anguishes over injustice. What a blessing to him when his people do what is right—when we treat people fairly and continually do good. Be encouraged that as you pursue righteousness, his goodness to you will be a refreshing stream that will never dry up.

How is God your referee?

CONTINUE IN CHRIST

Just as you received Christ Jesus as Lord, continue to live your lives in him, rooted and built up in him, strengthened in the faith as you were taught, and overflowing with thankfulness.

COLOSSIANS 2:6-7 NIV

Receiving Christ causes a wonderful transformation. But there is fullness to the Christian life that goes beyond salvation. The Scripture says that we continue our lives in him. This means that every day we have the opportunity to grow in our relationship with God.

As we develop our relationship with Christ, we experience a deep assurance of our faith and we are empowered to live a full life. It is easy to be thankful for all of the good things Jesus is doing in your life as you grow from strength to strength.

What have you been learning through God's holy Scriptures?

LEAN

Trust in the LORD with all your heart,
And lean not on your own understanding.

PROVERBS 3:5 NKJV

When we are faced with challenging situations, particularly when we are making big decisions, we often try to figure things out on our own. When that doesn't work, we start to pray. There's nothing wrong with this, but wouldn't it be better if we left it up to God in the first place?

God knows us intimately, and he knows our life situations. When we lean on God in times of need, the burden of trying to understand things in our own minds can be shifted to trusting in our hearts that God will work it out.

What decisions do you need to trust God with right now?

Walking in Works

We are His workmanship, created in Christ Jesus for good works, which God prepared beforehand so that we would walk in them.

EPHESIANS 2:10 NASB

God has always had a plan for your life. He created, designed, and brought you into being. He has gifted you with talents, nurtured you, and developed character in you as you have matured. You are his wonderful workmanship!

God knew from the beginning how to uniquely design you to empower you to do good works. Best of all, he created you in Christ Jesus, whose redemption and healing on the cross gave you all the grace that you need to walk in his ways.

What does walking in grace look like to you?

SATISFIED

Because your love is better than life,
my lips will glorify you.
I will praise you as long as I live,
and in your name I will lift up my hands.
I will be fully satisfied as with the richest of foods;
with singing lips my mouth will praise you.

PSALM 63:3-5 NIV

There are times in our lives when we really need answers or a breakthrough, and sometimes we just want to be blessed. Our loving Father says to simply ask.

God wants to give us good gifts. You might not want to ask for things because you feel they are too much, or too specific. But God is able to handle our requests—he won't give us things that will bring us harm or that we will use for our selfish gain. He knows what is best for us. His love is better than life itself, and he knows exactly how to satisfy us.

Can you define the difference between your wants and needs?

HOLY SPIRIT WORDS

"When you are brought into the synagogues before the leaders and other powerful people, don't worry about how to defend yourself or what to say. At that time the Holy Spirit will teach you what you must say."

LUKE 12:11-12 NCV

Defending our faith has always been a challenge. We might not be dragged into a court over our beliefs as some were in the apostle Paul's time, but we can expect to have opposition and confrontation about our faith.

The Holy Spirit was given to us as a helper. He fills us and reminds us of the words of Jesus. He brings Scripture to our mind. In those times when you need to defend the gospel of Jesus Christ, be confident that the Holy Spirit will give you the right words.

What can you say when you feel challenged to share or defend your faith?

EAST TO WEST

If I rise with the sun in the east
and settle in the west beyond the sea,
even there you would guide me.
With your right hand you would hold me.

PSALM 139:9-10 NCV

Moving on from anywhere can be disconcerting. A new circumstance, house, or even country means that we have to leave what we have been comfortable with and step out into the unknown.

Take courage that no matter where you go, the Lord will always go with you. He is as far east as the rising sun, and as far west as the sunset. He will guide you as you move, and he will hold you when you get there.

Is it hard for you to believe that God is with you wherever you go? Why or why not?

ASSIGNMENT

My life is worth nothing to me unless I use it for finishing the work assigned me by the Lord Jesus—the work of telling others the Good News about the wonderful grace of God.

ACTS 20:24 NLT

When it is all said and done, there is nothing more important in our lives than the good news of Jesus. He came to earth to reveal God's nature. He sacrificed his life to save us from our sin. He defeated death once and for all. He gave us a life of grace that we might walk in freedom. We have a lot of good news to share!

The joy of knowing good news is in being able to share it. Instead of spending your life trying to figure out exactly what you are supposed to be doing, remember the assignment that Jesus has given you—to tell others about his grace. This is an assignment worth finishing!

What is most important in this life?

WHOLE RESTORATION

My whole being, praise the LORD
and do not forget all his kindnesses.
He forgives all my sins
and heals all my diseases.

PSALM 103:2-3 NCV

Our God is a God of restoration. He shows us his kindness, through his love, in that he cares for our entire being. Not only does God want to restore a right relationship with you, he also wants to restore your body to health.

When we are spiritually or physically weak, we can sometimes forget the promises of God. In these times, think on his character; remember that he is a loving Father who wants the best for you. Praise him with all of your heart, soul, and mind, and watch him bring restoration to the areas of your life that need it the most.

What kindnesses of God do you remember today?

EQUIPPED FOR BATTLE

Put on the full armor of God,
so that you can take your stand against the devil's schemes.
EPHESIANS 6:11 NIV

At times it is hard to acknowledge that we are in a spiritual battle and that there is opposition to the good works of God. The devil does have his schemes, but God has provided us with everything we need to equip ourselves against these schemes.

We have the truth in the person of Jesus Christ. We have been granted salvation and righteousness through his grace. We have peace in the confidence of our eternal destiny. God's Word brings life. This is the armor that you can equip yourself with daily to be able to stand firm in your faith. Be strengthened!

What struggles can you face with God's truth, righteousness, and peace?

Prayer Counts

Pray in the Spirit on all occasions with all kinds of prayers and requests.
EPHESIANS 6:18 NIV

Often we are too analytical with our prayers. We think we ought to make them sound fancy or humble. We can treat prayer like money: we don't want to spend it on the wrong things. We might not be able to trust our intentions when we pray, but God sees our heart.

The Lord wants you to talk with him in all occasions and with all kinds of prayers. Sometimes our prayer is a quick cry for help, and sometimes it is an hour-long worship session! No matter what kind of prayer, Jesus will always be present to hear you.

How do you find yourself most often connecting with God?

Chased by Grace

Surely goodness and mercy shall follow me
All the days of my life;
And I will dwell in the house of the Lord
Forever.

PSALM 23:6 NKJV

We leave footprints as we walk along the journey of life. Some of these footprints are left from walking in the dirt and they need to be cleaned up because they don't belong to the path of righteousness.

God wants to lead you in the right direction. As you live in his ways your path will be followed by goodness, and his mercy will clean up those footsteps that have gone in the wrong direction. His grace will follow you all of your life. It is by this grace that you will dwell in the house of the Lord forever!

What kind of footprints is your life journey leaving?

Spiritual Guidance

If we live by the Spirit, let us also be guided by the Spirit.
GALATIANS 5:25 NRSV

Living by the Spirit means that we are continually dying to the sinful desires of our fallen nature. When we surrender our sinful nature to the cross, we produce fruit that is proof of the Spirit working within us. We see love, joy, peace, patience, kindness, goodness, faithfulness, gentleness, and self-control.

Not only can we see these fruits when we are living by the Spirit, but we can also use them to guide us in the right way. You will bring life into your situations and relationships when you give preference to the way of the Spirit.

What proof is there that the fruit of the Spirit is working in your life?

KEY TO SUCCESS

My child, do not forget my teaching,
but keep my commands in mind.
Then you will live a long time,
and your life will be successful.

PROVERBS 3:1-2 NCV

Today success is associated with riches and social status. Often, successful people have also had an academic advantage, having had access to good teachers and successful strategies to learning well.

In the same way, we are able to pursue Godly success through Godly wisdom and teaching. The teachings of Jesus are profound and life giving. We have an advantage in that the wisdom of God and his commands have been written down for us so we cannot forget. Study his Word and commit his teaching to memory, and you will have all that you need to live a full life in God!

What Godly success are you achieving right now?

A PATIENT PROMISE

The Lord is not slow about His promise, as some count slowness, but is patient toward you, not wishing for any to perish but for all to come to repentance.

2 PETER 3:9 NASB

Jesus will return one day—he promised he would! Until then, however, we live in the "in-between." The kingdom has come, but not in its fullness, and we await the time when the earth and everything in it will be restored.

Jesus' return can seem slow to those of us who are waiting, but if we understand the love that Jesus has for humanity, we can understand, in part, his timing for waiting for others to reach repentance. Praise Jesus for his love, and be patient in his promise. He will return!

What promises of God are you waiting to be fulfilled?

Pentecost Power

"You shall receive power when the Holy Spirit has come upon you;
and you shall be witnesses to Me in Jerusalem, and in all Judea and
Samaria, and to the end of the earth."

ACTS 1:8 NKJV

The Holy Spirit can be a powerful influence in your life if you learn
how to hear his voice. When the Holy Spirit came on the early church
believers, they witnessed many miracles, including being able to hear
each other speaking in other languages! Many people became Christians
as a result of these Holy Spirit moments!

When you genuinely display the power of the Holy Spirit, people will
be drawn to you and your witness of the gospel of Jesus Christ. Be
encouraged that the same Spirit that came upon the believers on that
day is with you today.

How is God's presence evident in your life?

HUMBLE HIGHS

Humble yourselves before the Lord, and he will lift you up.
JAMES 4:10 NIV

It seems an upside down thing to say—that in humility, rather than pride, you will be lifted up. Usually humility comes with a sense of shame. There is no shame, however, in humility before God. The Lord loves humility because it draws you close to him and allows him to work through you without having to battle your pride.

Humility before the Lord is the acknowledgement that you need his forgiveness, his grace, and his strength in all areas and at all times in your life. In your humility before him, he will encourage you, strengthen you, and lift you up!

How does pride get in the way of God speaking and working in your life?

FREE OF THE PAST

If anyone is in Christ, he is a new creation;
old things have passed away;
behold, all things have become new.

2 CORINTHIANS 5:17 NKJV

Before Christ, we were slaves to our sinful nature and had no freedom from the things we had done wrong. When Jesus Christ died on the cross, he took our sin upon himself. When he rose again, he displayed his victory over sin and death.

Your sins of the past belong to the old person, the one that did not have Christ. As Christians, we live by grace and in the forgiveness that God grants us because of Jesus' sacrifice. Live as the new creation God has made you to be, walking in the freedom of his grace.

What newness of life are you walking in?

STRENGTH OF HEART

Whom have I in heaven but you?
And earth has nothing I desire besides you.
My flesh and my heart may fail,
but God is the strength of my heart
and my portion forever.

PSALM 73:25-26 NIV

When God said, "I Am," he declared how all-encompassing his presence is, both in heaven and on earth. When we begin to understand both the love and the greatness of our God, we become convinced that he is everything.

The Lord is your all; there is nothing in heaven and earth that is greater. His love for you will give you everything you need. While everything else around you may fail and fall away, the knowledge of God will forever rest in your heart. He is your portion, forever.

Can you express your love for God today?

Convinced of Love

I am convinced that neither death, nor life, nor angels, nor rulers, nor things present, nor things to come, nor powers, nor height, nor depth, nor anything else in all creation, will be able to separate us from the love of God in Christ Jesus our Lord.

ROMANS 8:38-39 NRSV

Our relationship with Jesus Christ is eternal. You may have just begun this journey with him, or have been a friend of God for all of your life. Whatever your life story, you are covered by his grace and can never be separated from his love.

Jesus Christ is all about love for his people. He humbled himself and took on human form for you. He suffered rejection for you. He took himself to the cross and died for you. Nothing would have stopped his love for you. His love will surround you in the highest height and the deepest depth. Be convinced that nothing will separate you from the love you have found in Jesus.

**What things cause you to feel separated from God?
Can you apply the truth of God's Word to those things?**

OPPORTUNITY FOR JOY

When troubles of any kind come your way, consider it an opportunity for great joy. For you know that when your faith is tested, your endurance has a chance to grow.

JAMES 1:2-3 NLT

It's not easy to approach troubles with joy, unless we can understand how these things work out for good. One of the best things that comes from trouble is that we are tested. And while testing seems like something to get anxious about, when we pass, we have more confidence than we had before.

Endurance is a quality that is crucial to staying true to our faith in the hard times. Rather than giving up when troubles come, hold onto your faith in Jesus and ask the Holy Spirit to help you in times of trouble.

How is your endurance being tested?

QUENCHED

The desert and the parched land will be glad;
the wilderness will rejoice and blossom.

ISAIAH 35:1 NIV

There are times in life when we feel like we are always striving and never getting anywhere; where we thirst for something more but still feel dry. God has promised that there will be a day when we, the redeemed, will no longer thirst for fulfillment; when everything we desire will be satisfied.

Before that day, however, God is still willing and able to grant you an oasis in the desert and give you signs of life in whatever kind of "wilderness" you may be experiencing. Just like the promise Jesus made to the woman at the well, the water that he gives is everlasting and becomes in us a spring of water welling up to eternal life.

When do you draw from God's well of deep refreshment?

PROVISION

Now may He who supplies seed to the sower, and bread for food,
supply and multiply the seed you have sown and increase the fruits of
your righteousness.

2 CORINTHIANS 9:10 NKJV

The beginning of generosity is provision. Just as a farmer requires seed
for a harvest, we must also be provided with something to sow. God has
supplied you with everything you need to help in growing his kingdom.
He will increase your resources as you diligently plant the seeds of faith.

As God multiplies your resources, he will also increase the harvest,
that is, the good that comes from what you have sown. He gives to you
generously that you might be generous. Be encouraged to give from what
he has given you, and watch the blessings in your life increase.

**How can you sow seeds of faith so you see growth in your life
and in the lives of others?**

Light of the Dawn

Even in darkness light dawns for the upright,
for those who are gracious and compassionate and righteous.

PSALM 112:4 NIV

The middle of the night can be an anxious time to be awake, often bringing irrational fears of danger, disturbing thoughts, or a disquieted spirit. In contrast, the first rays of light in the morning can bring one peace, hope, and joy.

Life does not always seem full of hope and joy, especially when you have experienced hurt, anxiety, or depression. God's truth, however, is that even in your moments of darkness his light will dawn for you. Grace, compassion, and righteousness belong to you as you allow Jesus to shine his life into your heart.

How do you experience the hope and joy that comes with the dawn?

Heavenly Scent

Thanks be to God who always leads us in triumph in Christ,
and through us diffuses the fragrance of His knowledge in every place.

2 CORINTHIANS 2:14 NKJV

In ancient Rome, a triumph was a ceremonious procession granted to generals who had won a decisive victory in battle. Jesus Christ has triumphed over sin and death and we are called to be a part of this victory! He has led us in battle and we are on the winning side!

The victory of Jesus can be displayed in our words and actions, but it is also described as a perfume that diffuses into every place that we go. When you carry the confidence of your triumph, it will sit in the air around you and cause others to detect the fragrance of Jesus.

What have you been victorious over lately?

Thunder Theology

*"God's voice thunders in marvelous ways;
he does great things beyond our understanding."*

JOB 37:5 NIV

Thunder is powerful, mysterious, and commanding. It's little wonder that God's voice is described in this way. With his voice, he created the heavens and the earth. His voice can command all things into submission to his will.

Throughout history God has done great things, and he is able to do great things today. What are the great things that you have been asking for in your life? Do you believe that he can do them? Just like the thunder, we may not fully comprehend how God works, but we know that he is present and powerful. Trust him to do great things.

List some of the great things you have seen God do in your life.

SiMPLY BELiEViNG

These things I have written to you who believe in the name of the Son of God, that you may know that you have eternal life, and that you may continue to believe in the name of the Son of God.

1 JOHN 5:13 NKJV

When Jesus came to earth, there were many who saw him and witnessed his teaching and miracles, and yet did not believe. It is incredible that the belief in Jesus has carried on, long after he was taken back into heaven.

Jesus calls blessed those who have not seen him and yet believe. You are blessed because you love him and have faith in him. This is why you can have joy in the midst of all situations—because you have faith in the truth, and it will one day bring you to glory.

How can you believe even though you don't see God?

Fixed on Him

Looking to Jesus, the founder and perfecter of our faith, who for the joy that was set before him endured the cross, despising the shame, and is seated at the right hand of the throne of God.

HEBREWS 12:2 ESV

It is hard to imagine how Jesus endured such overwhelming suffering on the cross, but the Scripture explains that he looked towards the joy set before him. Jesus saw beyond his suffering for the purpose of our redemption, and he knew that God would be glorified.

In the same way, we are urged to look to Jesus. Some translations say that we "fix our eyes" on Jesus. This means that even when you are going through troubles of your own, you can focus on Jesus. Keeping our eyes on him allows us to see beyond our suffering and to know that God will ultimately be glorified as we keep our faith in him.

How do you fix your eyes on God so you see beyond your troubles and suffering?

ETERNAL KINGDOM

Since we are receiving a Kingdom that is unshakable, let us be thankful
and please God by worshiping him with holy fear and awe.

HEBREWS 12:28 NLT

Kings and queens hold their throne for a time, but ultimately their reign ends, either through defeat or death. The kingdom of God is not like the kingdom of men. It is undefeatable and unshakeable.

You belong to God's kingdom, and it will never be defeated. His power will not be surpassed by any other principality or power. Be thankful that you belong to this kingdom. Worship God as the king of this universe and the king of your heart!

How can you worship God in reverence and love?

Fiery Furnace

"If we are thrown into the blazing furnace, the God whom we serve is able to save us. He will rescue us from your power, Your Majesty."

DANIEL 3:17 NLT

What confidence Shadrach, Meshach, and Abednego had in God's power to rescue them from the blazing furnace! Not only did they refuse to worship the king's idol, they willingly went through the fire to prove the power of their God.

You are unlikely to have to go through literal flames for God, but he will honor your decision to stand up for your faith in him. You may feel pressured by the majority to live a certain way, to accept other religions, and to compromise your standards. Be encouraged that our God is the God who miraculously saved these faithful men from the fire, and he is the only one worthy of praise.

What idols do you need to take a stand against today?

EVERGREEN

Blessed are those who trust in the LORD,
whose trust is the LORD.
They shall be like a tree planted by water,
sending out its roots by the stream.

JEREMIAH 17:7 NRSV

Trees that are planted closest to the source of life are strong, healthy, and fruitful. In contrast, a tree that is not planted near water will struggle to survive when the heat or drought comes.

The Lord is your source of life! You will draw close to God as you pray, worship, read his Word, and fellowship with other believers. These are the roots you send out; they allow you to deepen your relationship with God. When you know you are close to the source, you will have confidence that through heat or drought, his refreshing waters are always available to sustain and bless you.

How can you plant yourself close to God?

My Redeemer Lives

"I know that my Redeemer lives,
and at the last he will stand upon the earth."
JOB 19:25 ESV

If you are familiar with the story of Job, you will know that God allowed him to suffer greatly; he lost his family, his health, and his wealth. We can empathize with Job as he wrestled with his understanding of God and the futility of life.

In the middle of suffering, the only thing that we may be able to hold on to is a declaration. While Job could not comprehend his suffering or God's ways, he knew in his heart and declared with his lips, "My Redeemer lives." Be uplifted as you dwell on that declaration. God is the one that ultimately has the final say for your life and for this earth, and you can boldly claim that he lives!

Who do you know that has demonstrated astounding faith in the midst of suffering?

Always Helping

God is not unjust; he will not forget your work and the love you have shown him as you have helped his people and continue to help them.

HEBREWS 6:10 NIV

Do you sometimes feel as though you give and give and are never appreciated? Women seem to have a natural tendency to help and care for those in need. Sometimes, though, this love towards others seems to go unrecognized and it can almost make us feel resentful.

While people may not take the time to appreciate your help, God most certainly will! He does not forget that you have shown love to his people, and he knows that this equates to your love for him. Keep up the good work!

How can you continue to do good work even without appreciation?

Rejoiced over

The LORD your God in your midst,
The Mighty One, will save;
He will rejoice over you with gladness,
He will quiet you with His love,
He will rejoice over you with singing.

ZEPHANIAH 3:17 NKJV

Parents are usually insanely proud of their children. It doesn't seem to matter what particular gift a child might have, a parent will always find something in that child to praise. A parent's love is not about what the child can do, but about who they are. They see a beautiful heart and amazing potential.

Our heavenly Father feels like this about us—only much more. Not only is he always present, he's protective, proud, and loving. Can you imagine him today, being so happy to be near you that he sings and rejoices over you! You are his daughter, and you are loved.

How does having a heavenly Father who delights in you so much help boost your confidence?

Many Wonders

Many, O LORD my God,
are the wonders you have done.
The things you planned for us.
None can compare with you;
were I to speak and tell of your deeds,
they would be too many to declare.

PSALM 40:5 NIV

It is good to give God the glory for all the things that are too wonderful for words. We know from the Bible that God has acted powerfully on many occasions to preserve his chosen people. We know that Jesus performed spectacular miracles. The Holy Spirit moved mightily on the early church and still shows his power today.

God didn't stop at making the earth; he continues to make wonderful things in this life. You can probably think of many examples of how God has done great things for you. Imagine how many believers can tell these stories as well… there are too many to declare!

What wonderful plans do you think God has in store for your life?

THIRSTY FOR MERCY

Come, all you who are thirsty,
come to the waters;
and you who have no money,
come, buy and eat!
Come, buy wine and milk
without money and without cost.

ISAIAH 55:1 NIV

Money is used for what we want, but mostly for the things that we need—like food and even water. Imagine walking into a grocery store and being offered anything you want without having to pay a cent! This is a picture of the mercy that Jesus has shown all of us through his sacrifice.

We need God's mercy in the same way that we thirst for water. Wine and milk were expensive items in the time this was written, and to offer these free of charge would have been a great sacrifice. What Christ did for you on the cross came at a great price, but it was all because of his great love for you.

What sacrifices do you make for those you love?

DIVINE DECISIONS

Oh, how great are God's riches and wisdom and knowledge!
How impossible it is for us to understand his decisions and his ways!
ROMANS 11:33 NLT

How do you know when you have made the right decision? When we are faced with uncertainty in a significant choice, we use a variety of strategies to come up with the right answer. Some of them are good reasoning, and others are not!

We should be careful not to project our decision-making difficulties onto the way the Lord makes decisions. The Bible says that his ways are not our ways and his thoughts are not our thoughts. God is rich with wisdom and knowledge; therefore, his ways are extremely superior to ours. Let him into your decision making process and trust his ways!

What decisions will you lay before God today?

CONTENTMENT

I know what it is to be in need, and I know what it is to have plenty. I have learned the secret of being content in any and every situation, whether well fed or hungry, whether living in plenty or in want.

PHILIPPIANS 4:12 NIV

What is the secret that Paul understood about contentment, and why would you need it in times of plenty? The shortcoming of both poverty and riches is that we always want more.

The secret to Paul's contentment was that he had experienced God's provision of his spiritual, emotional, and physical needs and knew that he didn't need anything more than trust in the Lord Jesus Christ. You don't need more to make you happy. Jesus is more than enough for you. Once you understand that, you can say, like Paul, that you have learned the secret of being content.

When have you experienced God's abundant provision?

Radiant Reflection

He is the radiance of the glory of God and the exact imprint of his nature, and he upholds the universe by the word of his power. After making purification for sins, he sat down at the right hand of the Majesty on high.

HEBREWS 1:3 ESV

Jesus was no ordinary man. We know this of course, but do we acknowledge Jesus as the divine being who had equality with God? When Jesus came to earth, he revealed God's nature to us. Because he is the radiance of God, he reflects a God that is both powerful and loving.

Though Jesus was divine, he came to earth as a man so that he could carry out the will of God. This was to be the ultimate sacrifice for all of humanity, so that our sins would be covered. Jesus, now seated with God in heaven, came for you. He upholds the universe, and he upholds you with his Word.

How can you walk in humility today?

Search Me

Search me, O God, and know my heart;
Try me and know my anxious thoughts;
And see if there be any hurtful way in me,
And lead me in the everlasting way.

PSALM 139:23-24 NASB

Searching requires looking in every place available to see what is there. Asking God to search your heart means that you are inviting him to know everything that is in it. Vulnerability is hard, particularly when we are battling pride or when we want to hide painful feelings or even sin.

Of course, God already knows your heart, so there is no point in hiding from him. But when you invite him in, you are acknowledging that you might need him to show you things in your heart and mind that need his love and guidance. Know that as you surrender to him, his love will cover all wrong, and he will lead you in the everlasting way.

**What anxious thoughts and hurtful ways
do you want to submit to God today?**

In his presence

Then I was constantly at his side.
I was filled with delight day after day,
rejoicing always in his presence.

PROVERBS 8:30 NIV

What does it mean to rejoice in the presence of God? To take delight in simply being with him? The natural outcome of being in God's presence constantly is joy, strength, delight, and a desire to remain there.

The more you soak in his Word and cultivate your relationship with him in your heart, the more he will delight you and satisfy you until you can do nothing but run into his presence daily with intense desire to be with him.

How do you crave God's presence?

INNER BEAUTY

Your beauty should come from within you—the beauty of a gentle and quiet spirit that will never be destroyed and is very precious to God.

1 PETER 3:4 NCV

God is enraptured by the inner beauty of your true self. It will never matter to him what you look like in the mirror as much as it matters to him what you look like in your soul.

Your face, your body, your weight; your human form is not what he fell in love with. The beauty of your spirit is what is precious to God.

How can you develop your inner beauty?

Returned Love

I love those who love me,
and those who seek me find me.

PROVERBS 8:17 NIV

With God, we never have to worry about being the one who bestows unrequited love. We always know, with absolute certainty, that our love—no matter how passionate—is even more passionately returned. God loves those who love him; he wants to be sought by you. But even more than that, he longs to be found by you.

Don't think that when you cry out to him you're speaking to thin air. He hears you and loves you. He gives himself to you. Continue in your love for him. Continue in your pursuit of him. He will give himself to you with even greater abandon than you can imagine.

What cries do you need God to hear today?

Continual Praise

From the rising of the sun to its going down
The LORD's name is to be praised.

PSALM 113:3 NKJV

What would it look like to be a woman who praises God from the time she awakens each morning until the time she falls asleep each night? Not only would we be pleasing God as we worship him constantly, but we would also effect an incredible change in our personal outlook.

Intentional, continual praise can only naturally result in intentional, continual joy. When I choose to look at each moment as a moment in which to be thankful and worshipful, then I will find in each moment beauty, joy, and satisfaction.

How can you be someone who continually praises God?

POWERFUL FRIENDSHIP

Flee the evil desires of youth and pursue righteousness, faith, love and peace, along with those who call on the Lord out of a pure heart.

2 TIMOTHY 2:22 NIV

The Christian life is revolutionary. We are consistently called to step out of the mold and live a life that is different. Being different isn't easy, but when we have other people around us who are living by the same revolutionary standard, we go from being odd to being impassioned.

Such is the power of friendship! In standing side by side, we can encourage one another to grow in our faith, and we can contagiously spread the message of Christ—the message of love and salvation—to the rest of the world.

Which of your friendships encourage you to love God more deeply and know him more fully?

OVERCOME

"I have told you these things, so that in me you may have peace.
In this world you will have trouble. But take heart!
I have overcome the world."

JOHN 16:33 NIV

It's so easy to feel overwhelmed by all of the evil in the world. But when we recognize the truth that our God has already conquered all of it, then we can have peace that is beyond anything imaginable.

The God who is on our side has—and always will have—the victory over all darkness. We can live our life with the strength and confidence that marks a true conqueror.

How do you walk in peace even in the face of adversity?

THE GOOD FATHER

"I will be a father to you,
and you shall be sons and daughters to me,"
says the Lord Almighty.
2 CORINTHIANS 6:18 ESV

We can easily confuse God's majesty with distance. We begin to think of him as someone who is out of touch with our daily lives—absent and uninterested. But the opposite is true!

God is a loving and kind father who takes interest in our deepest thoughts as a father does for his children. He loves us deeply and sensitively, as only a truly good father can. When we adjust our perception of God from far off to profoundly near, our intimacy with him can only deepen.

How can you adjust your perception of God?

RIGHT RELATIONSHIPS

**Above all, love each other deeply,
because love covers over a multitude of sins.**

1 PETER 4:8 NIV

Love is always the key ingredient in right relationships because love is synonymous with our creator, God. It was the spilled blood of love that blotted out the sins of man—and only that same love can allow two broken people to support one another in godly relationship.

When we strive to love one another deeply, we not only allow the very essence of Christ to flow through us, we also reveal him to the one we are in relationship with and to the observing world.

How can you love others deeply?

Joy that Testifies

Our mouths were filled with laughter,
our tongues with songs of joy.
Then it was said among the nations,
"The LORD has done great things for them."

PSALM 126:2 NIV

True, joyful worship testifies loudly of God's work in our lives. When we speak out in praise, with joy and laughter—because of what God has done for us—the rest of the world will take notice. Often, as Christians, we concentrate completely on walking forward in sober obedience, and we lose sight of the overwhelming joy of the Lord which is our strength.

When we take the time to praise and thank God with happy hearts, even those in the world cannot deny the evidence of God's great work.

How is God's joy evident in your life?

RELATIONSHIPS

Rejoice! Strive for full restoration, encourage one another,
be of one mind, live in peace.
And the God of love and peace will be with you.

2 CORINTHIANS 13:11 NIV

Engaging in healthy, godly relationships between believers is not easy—
especially when there is conflict. It can be almost automatic for us to run
the other way than to remain and face disagreements or repair a broken
relationship.

When we strive for unity and restoration, for encouragement of one
another and for peace, we are literally welcoming the very presence of
God into our relationships.

How can you fight for resolution in broken relationships today?

GRACIOUS

The LORD longs to be gracious to you;
therefore he will rise up to show you compassion.
For the LORD is a God of justice.
Blessed are all who wait for him!

ISAIAH 30:18 NIV

We can become so overwhelmed by our own shame, troubles, or misconceptions that we miss out on the most simple and beautiful truth—our God greatly desires to show us grace. He doesn't long to show us his anger or his punishment. He doesn't rise up to show us his power and his terrible greatness; he rises up to show us compassion.

When we enter God's presence with this point of view, we are humbled by his love despite his justice—because the punishment we deserve has been outweighed by the grace he longs to give.

How do you feel God's compassion toward you?

THE COMPARISON TRAP

Let each one examine his own work, and then he will have rejoicing in himself alone, and not in another. For each one shall bear his own load.

GALATIANS 6:4-5 NKJV

Comparison is an easy trap to fall into. When we hear someone else share their story, it can seem as though their life is going smoothly, with everything falling into place exactly as it should. Even when they share great difficulty, we hear their triumphs, making their lives seem far less complicated than our own.

But every single one of us has our dark, confused, and lost moments. And each of those moments will lead us to victory and pride in the work that God has done in us if we let it.

In what ways do you compare yourself to others?

FULL JOY

"So you have pain now; but I will see you again, and your hearts will rejoice, and no one will take your joy from you."

JOHN 16:22 NRSV

The joy that comes with the presence of the Lord is a joy that cannot be taken away. When we remember what Christ has done for us, and think about how his grace has changed the eternal course of our lives, we cannot help but be filled with an irrepressible joy.

We may struggle on difficult days, when our lives get hard, to keep sight of the joy of our salvation. But a day is coming when Jesus will return to this earth—setting all things right—and on that day, we will experience our joy in full.

How can you experience joy even on difficult days?

BOLD HOPE

Since, then, we have such a hope, we act with great boldness.
2 CORINTHIANS 3:12 NRSV

When we fix our eyes on the hope of salvation that we have in Christ Jesus, we cannot help but walk with bravery. When a soldier goes into a battle already knowing that he will come out as the victor, he is able to fight with unprecedented boldness.

As children of God, we are like that soldier. Our battle is already won for us—there is truly nothing to fear. We can walk bravely through life with the hope that makes us bold.

What do you need to walk bravely through right now?

God Who Searches

Thus says the LORD GOD: "Indeed I Myself will search for My sheep
and seek them out."
EZEKIEL 34:11 NKJV

God values his relationship with you so much that he is willing to go
to great lengths to capture your heart. He doesn't just sit stationary,
passively waiting for you to approach him. He says that he searches for
his sheep—seeking them out.

Have you ever consciously felt God's pursuit of you? Perhaps in
Scripture, in a sermon, in a song, or in the words of a friend? He speaks
to you because he cares so much about being with you. Allow yourself to
be pursued by your God, and respond to his pursuit with a heart that is
eager to be loved by him.

How have you felt God's pursuit of you?

Portion

"The LORD is my portion," says my soul,
"Therefore I have hope in Him."
LAMENTATIONS 3:24 NASB

We live in a world of consumerism where we are continually encouraged to want more. We are taught that with more things will come more joy. But the stuff of this life will never fill the hunger in our souls. The only proper sustenance for a weary soul is a great God.

The Lord is our portion—the perfect portion to fill our emptiness. We need nothing more than him to give us hope, direction, and a future. When we fill ourselves with him, there is nothing more we need.

What things can you pass along to someone who really needs them?

BROUGHT NEAR

In Christ Jesus you who once were far off have been brought near
by the blood of Christ.

EPHESIANS 2:13 NKJV

The redemption we have in Jesus has closed the gap that sin once created. We no longer are distant from God; we have been brought near as his children—drawn close in loving relationship.

By living in this truth we are able to cast off shame and formality, having been given the freedom to approach the throne of grace as those who have been redeemed.

How do you feel when you stand in God's presence?

ACCEPT IT

What we have received is not the spirit of the world, but the Spirit who is from God, so that we may understand what God has freely given us.

1 CORINTHIANS 2:12 NIV

The goodness of God toward us is so far beyond our human capacity for goodness that we struggle to understand it. Our difficulty in understanding God's gifts can ultimately lead to difficulty in our ability to accept them.

At salvation, God puts his spirit within us—enabling us to understand his love, mercy, and grace. With the spirit of God in us, we can both comprehend and accept in full what the Father has given to us.

What gifts from God do you need to accept?

ETERNAL LEGACY

The steadfast love of the LORD is from everlasting to everlasting
on those who fear him,
and his righteousness to children's children.

PSALM 103:17 NRSV

By putting our faith in Christ, we have entered into an eternal legacy of faith. With our hope and fear placed in God, we receive his steadfast love and his enduring promise. To be the recipient of a love that is everlasting means that you can never fall out of favor with the one who loves you.

Steadfast love doesn't change, doesn't run out, and doesn't lose its fervor. Rest in the fact that you are loved forever by the perfect lover.

What does steadfast love look like to you?

No Reason to Fear

Love the LORD, all you godly ones!
For the LORD protects those who are loyal to him,
but he harshly punishes the arrogant.
So be strong and courageous,
all you who put your hope in the LORD!

PSALM 31:23-24 NLT

Fear should not be a common emotion for a believer. When we live wholeheartedly in the truth that God has already won the victory for us, there is no reason to be afraid. God never leaves us alone and helpless. He is by our side through every situation we face—strengthening us to fight.

We can hold our heads high with courage and confidence in the knowledge that, with God by our side, we have no reason to fear.

What are you afraid of?

Diligent seekers

The soul of a lazy man desires, and has nothing;
But the soul of the diligent shall be made rich.
PROVERBS 13:4 NKJV

It is a dangerous thing to become comfortable with complacency in our Christian walk. When we are content to stay where we are in our relationship with God, we will not move forward in him. But when we set ourselves to motion in the pursuit of him, then we will be propelled forward in our faith.

If we want to truly know God, then our pursuit of him cannot be passive. We must call ourselves to action, becoming diligent seekers of his presence.

When you feel lazy, what do you do?

DWELLING PLACE

Do you not know that you are God's temple
and that God's Spirit dwells in you?

1 CORINTHIANS 3:16 ESV

A temple, by definition, is the place where God dwells. In the Old Testament, the people had to travel to the Tabernacle to offer sacrifices and worship God. They relied on a priest to enter the holy place and communicate with God on their behalf.

Under the new covenant, we have the Spirit of the living God dwelling inside our own bodies. At the moment of Christ's death, the curtain separating us from the holy place was ripped in two—symbolizing the end of man's separation from God. Now, his presence is with us always wherever we are, and his glory fills our very being.

How do you communicate with God?

TRUE LOVE

"All people will know that you are my followers if you love each other."
JOHN 13:35 NCV

We are commanded to love one another. But, love isn't easy. There are parts of every human relationship that are broken. Love is often about repair. You love each other past the difficulty and in spite of the inconvenience. True love is patient enough to rise above challenges and seek solutions. True love doesn't look to satisfy itself; true love gives.

When God defined love, he did it through sacrifice, demonstrating that there is no room for selfishness in love.

**How can you show selfless love and devotion
in your close relationships?**

Commissioned

"As Moses lifted up the serpent in the wilderness, even so must the Son of Man be lifted up; so that whoever believes will in Him have eternal life."

JOHN 3:14-15 NASB

Moses complied even with God's most awkward, uncomfortable commands. Once, he obediently constructed a brass snake, placed it on a pole, and ordered everyone to stare at it if bitten by deadly snakes. The Israelites must have scratched their heads, but the ones who actually trusted and looked to the snake were healed. This story foreshadows the sacrifice of Jesus on the cross: death came through the first Adam, yet salvation comes through the last Adam as we look to him in faith.

We have a commission similar to Moses': we lift Jesus high, telling people to look to him for eternal life. It may seem awkward, but we also set aside our self-awareness. We set before us Jesus Christ and his love for the people he came to save.

Do you feel equipped when you share your faith with others?

In the Race

> "Do not be afraid; you have done all this evil. Yet do not turn aside from following the Lord, but serve the Lord with all your heart."
>
> 1 SAMUEL 12:20 ESV

We often struggle, thinking we need to forgive ourselves because we lack peace about the sins of our past. The fact of the matter is this: Jesus' forgiveness is what is important, and if Jesus sets you free, you have no opinion in the matter any longer. Jesus forgave your sins. He brushes the dirt off your knees, kissing and bandaging your wounds. Now you can run again.

In running, never stop for the sake of hopelessness or doubt. Never take your hand off the plow because you feel unworthy. You never earned the right to serve God. Jesus is the one who bought you, and he is the one who forgave you. If the one who will judge all things has declared you clean, then you are a bride who is spotless.

How can you continue to serve God even when you feel unworthy?

REMEMBER

Those who love me, I will deliver;
I will protect those who know my name.
When they call to me, I will answer them;
I will be with them in trouble,
I will rescue them and honor them.

PSALM 91:14-15 NRSV

When we read God's Word, we glue our need to God's provision. We read the words on the page and realize God has helped people with the same needs as ours. Whether it's for love or wisdom, provision or righteousness, Jesus has all we need. He is a generous giver, and he has beckoned us closer to receive what he has for us—including intimacy with him.

Read through his Word and be trained of him. Let the Holy Spirit teach you all things as you ponder and reflect. Read the Psalms for comfort and encouragement; study the Proverbs for deeper wisdom. God's Word is written for you, and it belongs to you.

How are you growing your faith and learning from God's wisdom?

STRENGTH EVERY MORNING

Lord, be gracious to us;
we long for you.
Be our strength every morning,
our salvation in time of distress.

ISAIAH 33:2 NIV

In times of crisis, each new morning demands our strength. In seasons of difficulty, waking brings with it worry, fear, and distress. We all look for strength in different places; some of us find security in financial wellness, others in physical health, still others in community and friendships.

If Christ is the ultimate source of strength, then each new morning we will open his Word and find truth to counteract worry with peace, fear with understanding, and distress with steadfastness. His grace will make us more than able to rise each morning with strength for the day.

What do you need God's strength for today?

Unless the Lord

Unless the Lord builds a house,
the work of the builders is wasted.
Unless the Lord protects a city,
guarding it with sentries will do no good.

PSALM 127:1 NLT

To attempt any great work apart from Christ is meaningless. Without seeking to work alongside him in his will, our efforts are wasted and our goals are futile. But when we choose to partner with Almighty God in the work he is already accomplishing, then we experience the joy of his blessing and the reward of his presence.

Wait for God. Ask him to reveal to you where he is working and how he would like you to join him. Ask him to call on you as he did the disciples—by telling you to follow him and then by leading you directly into his will.

How can you be an effective participant in God's will?

Goodness in Waiting

The Lord is wonderfully good to those who wait for him, to those who seek for him. It is good both to hope and wait quietly for the salvation of the Lord.

LAMENTATIONS 3:25-26 TLB

Have you ever watched other people enjoy their "happily-ever-afters" while you sat wondering if yours would ever come? Sometimes it feels as though everyone else has their lives perfectly in order while your own is in some type of chaos.

Finding yourself waiting is challenging enough without watching everyone else rush ahead of you. But God promises goodness to those who are kept waiting. If you choose to seek the Lord as you wait, he will reveal himself to you in a sweeter way than you could have known otherwise.

What are you waiting on God for right now?

GRIT OF GRACE

Don't listen to everything people say,
or you might hear your servant insulting you.
You know that many times
you have insulted others.

ECCLESIASTES 7:21-22 NCV

There is something so awful about hearing that someone has spoken badly about you behind your back. You want a chance to defend yourself against such an unfair attack. But instead of quickly becoming angry, consider whether or not you have spoken similar negative words about someone else in the heat of a moment.

When we recognize our own failings, we free ourselves up to forgive even the most insensitive of offenders. It is in these moments that we come face to face with the grit of grace—understanding the depth of its reach and the extent of its value.

What is your definition of grace?

SIMPLY LISTEN

After the earthquake, there was a fire, but the LORD was not in the fire.
After the fire, there was a quiet, gentle sound.

1 KINGS 19:12 NCV

Hurricanes, tornadoes, tsunamis, and the like are sometimes referred to as acts of God. This means the occurrences were outside of human control, but the expression can lead us to misunderstand God and how he works.

Elijah knew exactly where to find God. After being told to wait in a cave for the presence of the Lord, he waited through a great wind, an earthquake, and a raging fire. Only after, when he heard a quiet, gentle sound, did he sense God's presence and go out to meet him.

Listen to God now. What is he telling you?

A GENEROUS HEART

A generous person will prosper;
whoever refreshes others will be refreshed.

PROVERBS 11:25 NIV

On the surface, this verse may seem to suggest that we give in order to get. Looking deeper, we see beyond. Think of a child reluctantly breaking a cookie into pieces, sizing them up, and handing over the smaller one with a scowl. The giver was most certainly not refreshed by this exchange.

Giving is an act; generosity is a condition of the heart. Only a generous heart is refreshed by giving. It is this generous heart our Father waits eagerly to bless.

How are you generous in your day-to-day life?

Sure Foundation

In that day he will be your sure foundation,
providing a rich store of salvation, wisdom, and knowledge.
The fear of the LORD will be your treasure.

ISAIAH 33:6 NLT

Think back to a time you were filled with fear. What caused you to feel unsafe? Whether from physical danger or emotional insecurity, you need never allow fear to take hold of you again.

Fear of the Lord, reverence for all he is and all he's done, replaces all fear. Once you have been saved by God's grace, once you know him and understand the foundation on which you stand, no power on earth can shake you. You are safe; you are his.

What do you think of when you consider God your "sure foundation"?

TRULY FREE

Out of my distress I called on the LORD;
the LORD answered me and set me free.

PSALM 118:5 ESV

Today, all across America, people celebrate freedom. At first glance, these gatherings may seem simply to relish the freedom to light fireworks, enjoy triple-berry pie, and inhale Aunt Mary's potato salad, but beneath the surface lies an opportunity for true worship.

As you wipe that tear from your eye during the National Anthem, consider what your freedom really means—not just as an American, but as an adopted daughter of the Almighty.

How can you thank God for setting you free from fear, sin, and death?

FOR HIS GLORY

I will do whatever you ask in my name,
so that the Father may be glorified in the Son.

JOHN 14:13 NIV

You have the power of Christ at your lips. How does this resonate with you? And how do you reconcile this incredible truth with seemingly unanswered prayers?

He promises to do whatever we ask in his name—in order to glorify the Father. Jesus sees well past today. Perhaps to truly bring glory to God we sometimes need an answer other than "yes," no matter how sincere our hearts and how worthy our requests.

What has God said no to lately?

NO PLAN B

> My victory and honor come from God alone.
> He is my refuge, a rock where no enemy can reach me.
>
> PSALM 62:7 NLT

When applying to colleges, students are invariably advised to have, in addition to their first choice—the place they really want to end up—a fallback school, a Plan B. It's less than ideal, but virtually guaranteed to work.

In matters of faith, God is the single source of our safety, our only means to victory. The good news: if we are truly his, we don't need a Plan B.

What is your Plan B?

In the Light

With You is the fountain of life;
In Your light we see light.

PSALM 36:9 NKJV

How would you explain color to a blind person? What is blue, and what makes it unique from red, purple, or green? In order to understand pink, you need to have experienced it.

It is the same with goodness, love, and light. In order to recognize it, we must know it. In order to know it, we must know the Father. He is the one true source of all light, of all that is good.

How do you see evidence of God's light around you?

PEACE IS MINE

May the Lord of peace himself give you peace at all times in every way.

2 THESSALONIANS 3:16 ESV

Think of a time when your life was absolutely perfect. How long did it last? Whether a moment, an hour, or even several days, eventually the shine wore off and real life crept back in. Here on earth, things will never be perfect.

This is why the peace of the Lord is such a valuable treasure! Jesus has overcome the world, so when we give him our hearts, his peace forms a barrier between us and everything that would steal our joy.

Have you wandered away from the peace of God? How can you get back?

BEST DAY EVER

A single day in your courts
is better than a thousand anywhere else!
I would rather be a gatekeeper in the house of my God
than live the good life in the homes of the wicked.

PSALM 84:10 NLT

Remember the best day of your life. Would you trade nearly three years of your life for that precious memory, let's say living to 85 instead of 88? Now magnify the greatness of that wonderful day beyond your imagining; picture a day in God's presence. How many ordinary days would that be worth?

Answer this next question thoughtfully: would you rather be poor, yet surrounded by people full of love and integrity, or wealthy among those who compromise morality and goodness as a matter of course?

How are you living a life that reflects your desire for God?

SUFFERING

He has graciously granted you the privilege not only of believing in
Christ, but of suffering for him as well.

PHILIPPIANS 1:29 NRSV

By its very definition, suffering is not enjoyable. Yet we are told that as
believers we are granted the privilege of suffering for Christ. Suffering as
a blessing? Something to be desired?

Consider what Christ suffered for us. Hard to imagine, isn't it? But if we
willingly place ourselves in difficult or painful situations in his name, we
draw a little closer. To experience pain while pursuing him is to know
more of his heart—a great privilege indeed.

What are you suffering through right now? Do you feel God's peace?

PERFECT PEACE

You will keep in perfect peace
all who trust in you,
all whose thoughts are fixed on you!
ISAIAH 26:3 NLT

What robs you of your peace? Thoughts of unpaid bills, unfavorable diagnoses, and unfulfilled dreams creep in unexpectedly, threatening the security we feel in our Lord's protection. But they don't have to.

These words in Isaiah are not a bargain: if we do this, he grants that. They are an observation. When we trust God fully, and keep our minds on him, we naturally feel peace. Because he is perfect, only perfect peace can come from trusting him. Thoughts fixed on him are thoughts steeped in tranquility.

When you trust God, what can you possibly fear?

STRONG ARMS

The everlasting God is your place of safety,
and his arms will hold you up forever.

DEUTERONOMY 33:27 NCV

In comedy, it's not uncommon to see a character lean against an unstable surface only to fall as they realize they misplaced their trust. What looked like a wall was actually a revolving door. Arms flail, legs fly, we laugh.

It's a little less funny when we're the ones flailing. God wants only stable surfaces for us to lean against, which is why we are called to trust him with all our hearts. Popularity, financial success, knowledge, and even relationships are ultimately just revolving doors.

How can you trust God's timing, plan, and provision over everything?

LIKE A CHILD

"Truly I tell you, anyone who will not receive the kingdom of God like a little child will never enter it."

MARK 10:15 NIV

Take a break from the mid-July heat and picture Christmas morning: children running down the stairs, tearing gleefully into packages. Every gift brings fresh exclamations of gratitude and joy. Each shiny ornament holds wonder.

This, we are told, is the only way to receive the kingdom of God. Like a child on Christmas morning, we must open up to wonder, enthusiasm, and thanks. How is this working in your life? Do you need his help in order to freely receive his gifts?

How can you be more childlike in your reception of God's kingdom?

By His Wounds

He was pierced for our transgressions,
he was crushed for our iniquities;
the punishment that brought us peace was on him,
and by his wounds we are healed.

ISAIAH 53:5 NIV

"I can't believe you did that for me!" Seldom do we feel more loved than when someone has gone through something—suffered—for us. How much, then, must Jesus love us?

No amount of suffering could truly be a fair exchange for all the world's sin, yet his pain was essential. Why? So we would feel the weight of it. The weight of our sin, and the weight of his great, great love.

How can you accept the healing God brings with his precious, perfect love?

RENEWAL

You were dead because of your sins and because your sinful nature was not yet cut away. Then God made you alive with Christ, for he forgave all our sins.

COLOSSIANS 2:13 NLT

As new Christians, we may naively think the transformation is permanent. We're his, therefore we're changed. While true, it's not the end of the story.

As long as we are here, we'll face temptation from the world. Renewal is an ongoing process. Each time we find ourselves conforming, we must re-transform, renew. What a blessing it is to know that we can. Again and again, he welcomes us.

What part of your thinking needs to be renewed?

Utterly authentic

> "Let the little children come to me, and do not hinder them,
> for the kingdom of God belongs to such as these."
>
> MARK 10:14 NIV

Jesus loved children. The Bible doesn't have many stories of him with children, but those we do have make it clear: he found them to be incredibly special.

What was it? Children have a way of just being, without any contrivance. Perhaps it was this authenticity. Maybe their absolute dependence was what captivated his heart.

In what ways do you recognize your need for God?

START HERE

The beginning of wisdom is this: Get wisdom.
Though it cost all you have, get understanding.
PROVERBS 4:7 NIV

If only all instructions were so straightforward: the first step on the path to wisdom? Realize how vital wisdom is. Understanding is worth everything we have. According to this verse, nothing matters more.

Let's take a moment to let this soak in. Without true understanding, everything we gain may be the wrong thing. No matter how successful or happy, or even how much good we do in the world, if we don't "get it," we may miss out on his plan—and nothing could possibly be worth that.

How do you pursue wisdom?

ASTOUNDING LOVE

"No, for I will give a sevenfold punishment to anyone who kills you."
Then the LORD put a mark on Cain to warn anyone
who might try to kill him.
GENESIS 4:15 NLT

This is God speaking to Cain. Yes, Cain. The murderer. He had just exiled him for his crime, but he also gave him protection.

God's love for us and his capacity to forgive us knows no boundaries. Anyone killing Cain could expect a punishment seven times more severe than the one Cain himself received for killing his own brother. That is love. And this is the God we serve!

What lengths would God go to in order to protect you?

Tribulation

I am filled with comfort. I am exceedingly joyful in all our tribulation.
2 CORINTHIANS 7:4 NKJV

Imagine being in prison. Now picture yourself joyful in prison. What would it take? Can you honestly imagine it? On our own, it would be impossible. The circumstances simply wouldn't allow it. But we are not alone.

The apostle Paul exemplifies many Christian attributes, but perhaps none more poignantly than joy. Joy is happiness regardless of circumstances—untouchable peace. It was Paul's, and it can be ours.

How can you be joyful in your trials?

SEEK HiS FACE

Seek the LORD and His strength;
Seek His face continually.

PSALM 105:4 NASB

Meeting someone in a crowd, we scan each face in search of their familiar features. Once we've found them, we feel relief, happiness, a sense of home.

This is the way our Lord wants to be sought. He desires not just presence or conversation with us, but intimacy. "Seek my face," he says. Not just forgiveness, not just answered prayer, but real, face-to-face connection.

How can you shift your focus from looking for things to looking for God?

TOTALLY COMMITTED

The LORD is faithful; he will strengthen you and guard you
from the evil one.

2 THESSALONIANS 3:3 NLT

Faithful friends never betray you. A faithful dog sticks close to your side. A faithful spouse has eyes only for you.

The Lord is faithful. Allow this incredible truth to strengthen and sustain you as you face whatever the enemy has planned today. God will never betray you; the creator of the universe never leaves your side; Jesus will never choose another over you.

How can you draw strength from the wellspring of God's faithfulness?

Take Refuge

Let all who take refuge in you be glad;
let them ever sing for joy.
Spread your protection over them,
that those who love your name may rejoice in you.

PSALM 5:11 NIV

Summer heat sometimes brings summer storms. With a tornado heading your way, you'd seek protection. You'd get low, beneath something sturdy and strong.

The Lord wants to be your shelter from the storms of life. He asks us to humble ourselves—to get low—before him and take refuge under his strong arms. The reward: not just protection, but songs of joy!

What storms are trying to rob your joy?

Abiding Love

Satisfy us in the morning with your unfailing love,
that we may sing for joy and be glad all our days.

PSALM 90:14 NIV

Think of brand-new love, where the newness and the enthusiasm are almost overwhelming. Whether a romance, a new pet, or even a new fitness plan, that feeling may or may not take root.

Let us make sure we are rooted in our relationship with Jesus. Has the joy of discovering him given way to the deeper joy of knowing him and walking with him each day?

How can you abide in God's love today?

Exposed

Nothing in all creation is hidden from God. Everything is naked and
exposed before his eyes, and he is the one to whom
we are accountable.

HEBREWS 4:13 NLT

Going through old family photos, we inevitably come across the "naked
and proud" photos. Babies and toddlers entirely exposed, and entirely
pleased with themselves. Adorable photos. We are utterly charmed.

Most of us have known a child like that. Some of us were a child like
that. Ponder this wonderful truth: you are still that child to God. There
is absolutely nothing about you he doesn't see and doesn't know, and he
finds you every bit as precious as a baby in a bathtub.

How do you think God sees you?

Friendship

Do not forsake your friend or a friend of your family,
and do not go to your relative's house when disaster strikes you—
better a neighbor nearby than a relative far away.

PROVERBS 27:10 NIV

Much is made of the importance of family, but the Bible makes it clear we are also meant to share our lives with friends. These are the people that are with you simply because you are you. What a precious and wonderful gift!

Loving, committed friendship with people in our communities is God's plan—and his gift—for us. Take care to nurture those relationships, and to be the kind of friend others seek out in a time of need.

What friends can you thank God for today?

HEART LONGING

My heart said of you, "Go, worship him."
So I come to worship you, Lord.

PSALM 27:8 NCV

When struggling with an important decision, we're often advised to listen to our hearts. The wisdom is that we already know what to do; when we tune into our longing, the answer is waiting.

With the Holy Spirit an active part of your life, your heart will often be directed toward the Lord. In times of need, in times of joy, listen to your heart and worship your God.

What is your heart longing for right now?

HOME

*"I will come back and take you to be with me
that you also may be where I am."*

JOHN 14:3 NIV

Where is home? For some, the place we came from will always be home. Others of us have found or created it in a new place, one of our own choosing. Maybe home isn't even a place for you, but a feeling you get with certain people.

Regardless of where we feel at home here on earth, the Lord wants us to remember our true home, which is in heaven with him. Those fleeting feelings of security and perfection are fleeting for just this reason. You are a citizen of heaven.

Where is your home?

LOST AND FOUND

I have gone astray like a lost sheep; seek Your servant,
For I do not forget Your commandments.

PSALM 119:176 NASB

The advent of GPS and smart phones has made it more rare, but still, occasionally, we may find ourselves lost. With no familiar landmarks and no one to follow, our only option is to ask for help.

We can lose sight of the route on our faith walk as well and find ourselves in that same predicament: lost. For spiritual disorientation, the same remedy exists: call for help.

How do you find yourself when you feel lost?

Watching

The Lord will watch over your coming and going
both now and forevermore.

PSALM 121:8 NIV

If you've ever been to a park with a small child, you know this one thing: don't take your eyes off them. Both danger and delight lurk on every swing, every slide. Other children may be new friends, or may throw sand in your little charge's face. You have to be there, watching.

To God, you are that child. Your Abba never takes his eyes off you. He wants you to experience swinging high, making friends, and climbing ladders. You'll get a few scrapes and bruises, but because he is with you, you'll be okay.

How do you feel God watching over you today?

Prepared in Advance

There is surely a future hope for you,
and your hope will not be cut off.
PROVERBS 23:18 NIV

God made you. Carefully, intentionally, he made you. And he knew exactly what he was doing, and why. Even the desires of your heart are there on purpose: to lead the Father's plan for your life.

The next time you doubt your worth, remember these words. The next time your question your purpose, look to your passions. What wonderful things did he prepare in advance for you to do?

What do you most doubt about your abilities?
Can you trust that God has prepared wonderful things for you?

ALL FOR GOOD

"You intended to harm me, but God intended it all for good.
He brought me to this position so I could save the lives
of many people."

GENESIS 50:20 NLT

We don't like thinking about this, but sometimes we have to go through horrible things to become the person God wants us to be. We can't always see past "now," especially when it's hard, to realize that rather than happening to us, our circumstances are leading us to where we need to be.

Even in the wake of unspeakable tragedy, the Lord leads us through, holds us close, and shapes us into who we're meant to be. Within God's perfect plan, even other people's sins against us can be used for good.

How has God made your life beautiful?

TO THE MOUNTAINS

I lift up my eyes to the mountains—
where does my help come from?
My help comes from the LORD,
the Maker of heaven and earth.

PSALM 121:1-2 NIV

It would seem that the psalmist is tapping into a tendency that we have—to look somewhere other than God for help. We might even be looking at grand, promising entities like a mountain. When someone is desperate for strength, their eyes can frantically search around for something, anything, to offer them help.

Have you looked to the mountain? Did it offer you anything? Did it save you or strengthen you? The psalmist immediately answers that question: help comes from the Lord. And then he goes on to unpack why the Lord is more supreme than a mountain—he's the maker of the mountain. And he's the maker of heaven and earth. Don't look to the created; look to the creator for help. You will not be left in want.

Where do you find your help?

SEEK AND FIND

"Keep on asking, and you will receive what you ask for. Keep on seeking, and you will find. Keep on knocking, and the door will be opened to you."

LUKE 11:9 NLT

Have you ever sought after something with no guarantee of a return? Maybe you participated in an Easter egg hunt as a child and went away empty handed, or took an ocean tour boat with the hope of seeing whales but returned to the dock with only the sight of sea waves banging against your ship. We are prone to seek after many prizes, but few treasure hunts will guarantee any return on your dollar or your time.

There is one treasure hunt you can guarantee will leave you fulfilled. Seek God and you will find him. He promises this in his Word. You can know with certainty that any investment you make in seeking him will be rewarded.

How can you boldly approach God to find help in your hour of need?

CASTING

Cast all your anxiety on him because he cares for you.
1 PETER 5:7 NIV

We are boldly called to do something that is entirely unnatural. Cast our anxieties on the Lord? What a word! Have you ever been anxious? Have you ever been paralyzed with fear? What should we do as God's children? His advice is simple. Cast it to him.

Casting means to throw out aggressively. Sometimes we habitually turn into anxious people, facing every trial with fear and not our promised peace. In training yourself to be a "caster" of anxiety and not a holder of it, you will enjoy abundant freedom that you had previously only wished for.

**How can you break the habit of anxiety
and learn to enjoy the freedom God gives?**

Delivered from Fear

I sought the Lord, and he answered me
and delivered me from all my fears.
PSALM 34:4 ESV

For various reasons, many of us grow up with certain fears in our hearts. Often the fear is unwarranted, but sometimes it's based on tragic circumstances. When fear's seeds sink into our hearts, they can grow giant trees of debilitating behaviors that paralyze us from functioning normally.

Praise the Lord that we have an advocate who has the power to demolish every stronghold and fear that has ever gripped us. The simple formula to access the power of our deliverer is to seek him. God's job is to deliver; our role is to seek. Seeking takes perseverance and endurance, but as we do, we can rest in the promise of his Word that he will indeed deliver us from all our fears.

What does it mean to persevere in seeking and trusting God for healing?

BURiED TALENTS

"Whoever has will be given more, and they will have an abundance.
Whoever does not have, even what they have will be taken
from them."

MATHEW 25:29 NIV

God, in his well-executed plan, endowed his children with talents. In Matthew 25:15, we get a small glimpse of his purpose in putting unique gifts within each of us. God alone decides how many talents he will entrust us with. These talents are graciously endowed to us and are not actually meant for our own benefit; they are intended to be a blessing to others.

Is the thought of exercising your talents so overwhelming in your already hectic schedule that you have chosen to bury them instead? Buried talents do nobody any good. Exercising those talents will actually become life giving to you.

How are you created to serve?

Thorns

In order to keep me from becoming conceited, I was given a thorn in my flesh... Three times I pleaded with the Lord to take it away from me.
2 CORINTHIANS 12:7-8 NIV

Would you like some great news today? Every child of God is profoundly imperfect. In addition to being imperfect, we all have besetting weaknesses. Many of these weaknesses can be managed and some, through the power of God, can actually be healed. But rest assured, weaknesses will not altogether go away. Once one is conquered, you will often find that another gets exposed. They are part of humanity.

What is your thorn? What area do you wrestle in continually? Paul, the great hero of our faith, also wrestled with a besetting weakness. God wants us to remain weak so that we can be strong in him. We are forced to remain in the place of humility, clinging to God for strength and comfort.

What is the thorn in your flesh?
Do you continue to ask God to take it away?

True Strength

I pray that from his glorious, unlimited resources he will empower you with inner strength through his Spirit. Then Christ will make his home in your hearts as you trust in him. Your roots will grow down into God's love and keep you strong.

EPHESIANS 3:16-17 NLT

Do you know today that God has not asked you to be strong? You won't hear that from TV, magazines, or social media. God didn't make you to be a model of your strength for others. He did make you to be a model of his strength though.

There is a big difference between being strong in our own power and being strong in God's power. The key to strength in God starts with acknowledging our profound weaknesses. When we own our weakness, it is an act of humility. God never asks us to be strong; he wants us to be dependent on him. Someone who is humble and dependent gets the gift of God's supernatural strength.

Can you find God's strength in your weakness?

EXTRAVAGANCE

In the last days I will pour out my Spirit on all kinds of people.
ACTS 2:17 NCV

Sometimes visual aids help us understand a concept that would otherwise be lost. Did you pour anything this morning? Milk on cereal, water on plants, creamer in coffee, or bathwater on a child's head? Pouring is very different than dripping. It's more than a small steady stream of liquid. Pouring indicates something gushing from a source. It is an unleashing that saturates.

God uses the same terminology of what he does when he gives his Spirit. He says he pours it out. God knows that you don't just need a trickle or a sprinkling of his Spirit. He delights in pouring more of himself over you as you ask and wait. It is his delight and his gift to you—and it will never run out.

When have you felt the extravagance of God?

HEARING TRUTH

"When he, the Spirit of truth, comes, he will guide you into all truth."
JOHN 16:13 NIV

Do you have a steady diet of truth-hearing in your life? Whether we like it or not, every one of us in varying degrees is constantly hearing ungodly wisdom. The world will not counsel you in the ways of God. It will urge you to hate your body, hold a grudge, and accept every sin under the sun. These messages will be spoken loudly.

It is of utmost importance to regularly hear, read, and meditate on truth. It won't always be natural to remember or believe, so it is critical that we daily refresh our mind and our spirit with it.

In what areas do you need to think less like the world and more like God?

ANCHORED SOUL

Then you will experience God's peace, which exceeds anything we can understand. His peace will guard your hearts and minds as you live in Christ Jesus.

PHILIPPIANS 4:7 NLT

No matter how uncertain your future may be, or how confusing your circumstances, your life is firmly established on the faithfulness of God. Nothing can shake you when your eternity is secured.

The peace that is available to the heart of a believer is beyond our human understanding. When we have the peace of Christ, we cannot be shaken to our core. We may feel overwhelmed, and we may even begin to lose our faith, but deep within us our souls are anchored and cannot be moved.

How do you allow God's peace to guard your heart?

Finishing Touches

Looking unto Jesus, the author and finisher of our faith.

HEBREWS 12:2 NKJV

Have you ever watched an artist paint a picture? The artist begins with an unblemished white canvas waiting to be transformed into a piece of art. As you watch, at different times it seems as if the painting could be finished. But in the last few moments, the artist applies the fine detail and extra colors that make the painting truly complete.

God is also a finisher. Our faith begins with God as the author. As we walk with him, we find ourselves believing that once he gets the ball rolling, it's up to us to finish the task. Praise the Lord that he declares it is his responsibility to not only author our faith but also to finish it. Don't walk away before he is finished! Those final touches can make a precious masterpiece.

What are you waiting for God to complete in you?

JUST RUN

Let us also lay aside every weight and the sin that clings so closely.

HEBREWS 12:1 NRSV

Have you ever observed the clinging power of a used dryer sheet? When a load of laundry is complete, the used dryer sheet is often stuck to a piece of clothing so tightly that it looks like it has been sewn on top of it. However, simply pulling on a corner of that clinging dryer sheet will remove it.

The nature of sin is to cling to us and grip us. Like a dryer sheet, sin won't simply fall off us. It takes an intentional action to remove or resist it. But it can be conquered. If you are casually swiping away the sin in your life, perhaps it's time for a different approach. Maybe it's time to run from the sin and into God's presence.

What sin is trying to cling to you?
Can you lay it aside and run into God's presence?

AUGUST 13

DIVINE CITIZENSHIP

He has granted to us his precious and very great promises,
so that through them you may become partakers of the divine nature,
having escaped from the corruption that is in the world.

2 PETER 1:3-4 ESV

Do you remember where you were on September 11, 2001? Not since
December 7, 1941, at Pearl Harbor, had we seen an attack on American
soil. Sure, we had fought in wars since that date, but the wars were
always in another country. September 11 showed us that we weren't
invincible to an enemy attack—and our epicenter of commerce and
trade could be deeply shaken.

This is one of the reasons it is important to rejoice that while many of us
might be Americans, it is not our only citizenship. If we have given our
lives to God, we have become citizens of his kingdom. We do not know
what will happen in America, or around the globe, in the next 100 years.
There might be much more shaking to come. But if our hope isn't set on
our earthly nation, we will be okay.

How do you feel about your citizenship in God's divine kingdom?

Gift of Song

Praise the Lord!
Sing to the Lord a new song,
his praise in the assembly of the godly!
PSALM 149:1 ESV

Some of us are singers and some aren't. Some have been given a pitch-perfect voice, and others are embarrassed to sing too loudly for fear that hearers will cringe. Regardless of which camp you land in, God still gives you the gift of song.

All throughout Scripture we are encouraged to sing to God... a new song. He wants us to sing a song that hasn't been written by someone else, but one that is sung from our heart to his. Singing to God is an act of worship that delights God regardless of your vocal ability.

Write a song of worship to God.

PARENTAL WORDS

You are precious in my eyes,
and honored, and I love you.

ISAIAH 43:4 ESV

Parental words carry much power. If life-giving, those words help us face our greatest fears with added strength. We feel as if we can take on the world. The converse can be true as well. If the words we heard from our parents were full of defeat and discouragement, it might be hard to silence those words when we are trying to conquer obstacles.

For a child of God, there is a parental voice that carries more weight and power than that of our earthly parents. Being born of his will and not just the will of our parents, we have a truly supreme parent in God. So, receive his words of life to you. Know that you are precious to your Daddy and he loves you.

How is your view of God shaped by the view of your parents?

WASHED AWAY

"Already you are clean because of the word that I have spoken to you."
JOHN 15:3 ESV

There are many options for trying to get stains out of clothes. Some will come out with a simple wash in the machine. Others require a special soaking product, and still others can be removed by scrubbing the fabric repeatedly. But have you ever had a stain that couldn't be removed? After you tried everything, you had to accept the fact that the stain was there to stay.

As Christians, we can become stained by the world through our own sin. Many of us try to use every method under the sun to feel clean again, but God's solution is simple. When you come to him in repentance, he himself will make you clean.

What stains do you want removed from your life?

TROUBLE

The righteous person faces many troubles,
but the LORD comes to the rescue each time.

PSALM 34:19 NLT

Jesus, knowing exactly what his disciples needed to hear before he died, gave them lots of counsel. He knew they did not fully understand that he was getting ready to suffer. He wanted to make sure their theology accepted that even in the life of a believer—even in his life—suffering would be included. They would not be immune to it.

Indeed we will have troubles of many kinds, but we shouldn't be dismayed or surprised by them. God has not forgotten us or forsaken us. It is simply part of living here on earth. We might see dimly now, but God did overcome evil, and we will see his completed work in all its glory when we stand in his presence.

What do you need from God today?

FLiCKERS

"My kingdom does not belong to this world."
JOHN 18:36 NCV

If you consume a regular diet of nightly news, it might be easy for you to become depressed. Wickedness seems to prevail, and some of the most heinous crimes continue to be committed. There are stories of corruption in our government and schools: institutions that are meant to be a stabilizing force in our communities.

Jesus makes it clear that we won't see his kingdom fully expressed here on earth. He is building a kingdom that cannot be shaken, but it isn't our government or our current social institutions. We might see little flickers of godliness in these places, but they are not his kingdom. His kingdom is coming and it will never end.

Write down your thoughts about God's kingdom.

In the Love

Keep yourselves in God's love as you wait for the Lord Jesus Christ
with his mercy to give you life forever.

JUDE 1:21 NCV

It's a simple but profound admonition. "Keep yourselves in God's love."
What does it mean to keep yourself in God's love? Perhaps it's easier to
picture what it doesn't mean. A heart that isn't in God's love is a heart
that is accusatory and angry. When it sees calamity or suffering, instead
of trusting that God is still love, it accuses him of being cruel and distant.

Nothing delights God more than a heart of faith that says, "Despite what
I might see or experience, I still believe that you are a God of love." Our
temptation will be to leave the love of God when we face hardship. That
is why we are admonished to keep ourselves there, even if it takes all of
our strength to do so.

How do you remain in God's love?

Becoming Childlike

"Truly I tell you, unless you change and become like little children,
you will never enter the kingdom of heaven."

MATTHEW 18:3 NIV

Much of our childhood is spent preparing to be adults. Our parents wouldn't have been doing their jobs well if they encouraged us to remain like children. Instead, they spent hours training us to be successful adults.

God's job as our Father is different. In our spiritual journey, he doesn't want us to become like adults. If we do, we have to fight to become like children again. What is it about children that we need to become like them in our faith? It would appear to be their humility. Children aren't arrogant or self-sufficient: they happily receive provision from their parents. God beckons us to resist proud, adult-like tendencies and happily submit to his leadership and provision.

How can you become like a child in your faith?

NOT WORTH COMPARING

I consider that our present sufferings are not worth comparing
with the glory that will be revealed in us.

ROMANS 8:18 NIV

Are you suffering today? Is this a week of suffering or an entire season?
The disciples that have gone before us, even those who walked with Jesus
himself, all suffered: some as martyrs unto death, some watching their
loved ones die, and others being shunned from their families because of
their faith.

Paul knew suffering intimately, so his words should be of great courage
to you. Our current suffering isn't even worth comparing to the glory
that will be revealed. That glory of his coming kingdom will be so
glorious that your current trial will pale in comparison. Find courage to
keep pressing on, knowing that there is a glory that will far surpass your
current pain.

What are you suffering with right now?
Do you feel hope when you think about eternity?

REJOICE IN TROUBLE

We can rejoice, too, when we run into problems and trials,
for we know that they help us develop endurance.

ROMANS 5:3 NLT

God clearly tells us there is more to do in our sufferings than suffer. He calls us to rejoice. Thankfully, we immediately get a picture of what we are to be rejoicing about. God allows suffering for many different reasons—most of which we won't necessarily understand in this age. But one that we might be able to wrap our minds around is that suffering produces something good: endurance. Endurance is what allows us to go further than we once did.

Those who endure well are those who have suffered well. Endurance grows through trial and tribulation—not when things are easy. Let's not despise our trials; let's thank God that they are producing great endurance in us that will lead to character and hope.

How can you rejoice in your suffering?

Feeding on Faithfulness

Trust in the Lord, and do good;
Dwell in the land, and feed on His faithfulness.

PSALM 37:3 NKJV

The person who trusts in the Lord has a beautiful life. Our trust in him alleviates all the natural tensions of our daily lives. We can be at peace knowing God will faithfully care for all of our needs. Our responsibility is just to do what is good in the land, rest in Christ, and enjoy the faithfulness of our Heavenly Father.

We simply must feed on his provisional care. When we meditate on his faithfulness, our stresses will be relieved, and we will enter a state of rest that can only be known by the true believer.

What opportunities do you have to do good on the earth?

Not Without Hope

We were given this hope when we were saved. (If we already have something, we don't need to hope for it. But if we look forward to something we don't yet have, we must wait patiently and confidently.)

ROMANS 8:24-25 NLT

When you chose to trust God with your life, you did it in hope. No one gives their life to God expecting or hoping in nothing. You hope that the new life he gives you will be better than your present life. You hope that you will one day see him face to face. You hope that he will take your life and use it for his glory.

As Paul articulates, for something to be truly hoped for, we cannot already possess it. If we have it, then there is no need to hope for it. True hope rests in the belief and trust that something will come to pass. This isn't foolishness; it is Biblical. Have you grown weary in hoping? Approach God again, in the same hope you had when you were first saved.

What do you need courage for today?

Continual Intercession

Who can say God's people are guilty? No one, because Christ Jesus died, but he was also raised from the dead, and now he is on God's right side, appealing to God for us.

ROMANS 8:34 NCV

Did you grow up with parents that prayed for you? Some of the most comforting words a child can ever hear are a parent's prayers. Not all of us had parents that prayed. Furthermore, some of those parents that once prayed may have gone on to heaven.

Take heart. There is still one who is praying. Perhaps your earthly parents aren't praying. That's alright. Someone who will always have the Father's ear is continually making intercession for you as he sits by God. His name is Jesus, and your name is written on the palm of his hand.

What do you think Jesus prays for you about before the Father?

Strong Faith

Faith comes from what is heard,
and what is heard comes though the words of Christ.
ROMANS 10:17 NRSV

Who are your heroes of the faith? What are some of the distinctions about them that you notice? People who have a deep faith in God are inspiring to us all. They remind us that no trial can consume us, that God is still there even when he seems distant. They seem unwavering in their walk when our feet feel unsteady.

Where does their faith come from? According to this verse, faith is grown largely from hearing the Word of Christ. It is hard to believe in promises that you don't even know exist. It is hard to trust in God's attributes and character if you haven't seen them yourself in Scripture. Don't forsake time in God's Word. Your faith will grow from hearing and believing it.

How does faith come from hearing the Word of God?

Near

The LORD is near to the brokenhearted,
and saves the crushed in spirit.

PSALM 34:18 NRSV

Have you ever been brokenhearted? What broke your heart? Was it a person? A circumstance that you couldn't change? Being brokenhearted is no small thing. It is not mere discouragement; it is severe pain. Pain that is hard to bounce back or recover from. There is little that can be done for those who are truly brokenhearted. And sometimes those who are very close get pushed away.

There is one who is allowed to go near a brokenhearted person: one that is not put off by rejection or grief. Isn't it a marvelous truth that the Lord is able to draw near to the brokenhearted. He is not kept at bay like others might be. This is because he alone is fully equipped to bear their pain. Are you brokenhearted or trying to comfort one who is? Go to God. He is already nearer to you than you realize.

How have you seen God move when your heart has been broken?

SUPERHUMAN

May he give you the power to accomplish all the good things your faith prompts you to do.

2 THESSALONIANS 1:11 NLT

God isn't asking you to be superhuman. Perhaps others are. Perhaps there are expectations placed on you that are unreasonable or unattainable. If that is the case, please don't exhaust yourself trying to be someone that you can't be.

God knows your frame. He is your maker and your designer. He didn't give you an indestructible body like his. He made you from dust and you will one day return to being dust. He knows that you are innately weak and your body will fail. This shouldn't discourage you. Take great heart that he doesn't expect you to be or act like him. He will give you an indestructible resurrected body one day. Today, your frame is one that will return to dust. This is a hopeful truth because it allows you to draw your strength from the one who is superhuman. His strength is yours when you lean on him.

Why is it important not to strive to be superhuman?

STEADFAST LOVE

As high as the heavens are above the earth,
so great is his steadfast love toward those who fear him.
PSALM 103:11 ESV

Let's take a moment to contemplate steadfast love. Steadfast love is steady. It doesn't get offended easily. It can weather incredible relational strain. It can handle faithlessness. It won't quit even when the recipient's love has grown cold.

This is steadfast love. And this is how God describes his love toward his children. He promises fidelity and faithful love even when you aren't faithful to him. If you run from him, upon your repentance he stands ready to accept you and pour more of his steadfast love upon you. He won't charge you for it or remind you of your weakness. He will simply strengthen you.

What do the words steadfast love mean to you?

WORTHLESS THINGS

Turn my eyes from looking at worthless things;
and give me life in your ways.
PSALM 119:37 ESV

Does social media call your name throughout your day? There is no doubt that it can be a gift from God. It can hold encouragement for you that you otherwise would not have seen. It can alert you to a prayer need that is urgent. And it can remind you of a loved one's birthday.

There is also no denying that it can be a colossal waste of time. There are worthless things all over our social media outlets. We are not alone in our struggle to resist looking at those things. Even in the days before Christ, people were tempted to waste their time on worthless cares. God wants us to have life, and that comes as we walk in his ways.

What worthless things do you want to turn away from?

GROWING WEARY

Let us not grow weary of doing good, for in due season we will reap,
if we do not give up.

GALATIANS 6:9 ESV

A time-tested principle is that you reap what you sow. Apart from any environmental upheaval, if you plant corn, you will reap corn. If you plant soy beans, you will reap soy beans. You can confidently sow a row of spinach and not be weary of cauliflower growing in its place. Cauliflower won't grow because you didn't sow cauliflower seeds.

That same principle applies to sowing seeds of goodness. If you sow seeds of goodness like forgiveness, gentleness, and honesty, you are guaranteed to reap the fruit of those seeds. There is one trick—don't give up. Don't plan to reap something that you just started sowing. Maybe you will see fruit immediately from the good seeds you planted, but in most cases, it takes years. Rest assured, you will eventually reap the seeds of goodness if you don't give up.

What do you need God's strength for today?

A BASKET CASE

"I took the load off their shoulders;
I let them put down their baskets."

PSALM 81:6 NCV

People in developing countries typically have few options when a heavy load of some kind must be moved. In Africa, a tribal woman can carry up to 70% of her body weight on the top of her head. Physical burdens are—yes—burdensome and require strength and stamina.

Spiritual and emotional burdens are the same. The heaviness and fatigue of the soul can bring depression and even a loss of hope. There is great news. We have a burden bearer—one who is well equipped and ready to remove our hands from our heavy load. Our responsibility is to let him do it. Put all of your concerns, worries, fears, and doubts into God's mighty basket and let him haul it away. You don't have to be a basket case!

What do you need to put in God's basket today?

NOT HIDDEN

"You are the light of the world. A city set on a hill cannot be hidden."
MATTHEW 5:14 ESV

Lights from major cities like Los Angeles, Nashville, and Atlanta can be seen from space. In fact, their brilliance increases 50% more during the holiday season! These cities simply cannot be hidden.

As believers, we are to be a light, shining for all to see. If there ever was a time in history where the beacon of light needed to illumine the darkness, it is now. We dare not hide behind the façade of political correctness and fear, but rather speak and live in the luminance of Christ's truth. We have the light of the world living in us and we know the truth that sets us free.

What helps you shine brightly in this dark world?

Bad News

They will have no fear of bad news;
their hearts are steadfast, trusting in the LORD.
PSALM 112:7 NIV

In this age of technology, we can be inundated with happenings from around the world. News is always at our fingertips—and often it's not good. Sometimes we are waiting for the personal, life-changing kind of news: the medical report, the upshot of the job interview, the test score. Our fear is that the result will not be what we hope.

Psalm 112 tells us that we do not have to fear bad news. If our hearts are righteous, we are steadfast and secure. In spite of any alarming information coming our way, we can be at peace because we are safe in God's hands.

**What fears tend to take over your mind?
Can you give them to God today?**

BLOOM

"They are those who, hearing the word, hold it fast in an honest and good heart, and bear fruit with patience."

LUKE 8:15 ESV

Most of us want to make a significant mark somewhere in our lifetime. It's comforting to believe that the routine of our ordinary lives is merely preparation for the really big assignment that surely is just around the corner. You know, the lofty thing, the high calling, the noble assignment that undoubtedly is directly ahead.

Then one day in a moment of quiet, the Lord whispers, "This is it. What you are doing is what I've called you to do. Do your work, raise your kids, love your neighbor, serve people, seek me first, and everything in your heart you long for will be fulfilled. Be faithful right where I've put you. You don't need to accomplish great things for me. Just be."

What makes you significant to God?

BLACKBIRD BLUFF

Stay alert! Watch out for your great enemy, the devil. He prowls around like a roaring lion, looking for someone to devour. Stand firm against him, and be strong in your faith.

1 PETER 5:8-9 NLT

In the parking lot of a lovely little park, a sleek blackbird demanded attention. He was busy pecking at a small wad of bread. A much larger blackbird circled him menacingly—moving in closer, then hopping back. You could almost hear his bird voice squawking, "Drop it buddy, and I mean now!" The smaller bird seemed completely oblivious. He was not in the least frightened, and he continued to enjoy his dinner. After a moment, the bully bird backed off. He was suddenly the same size as the other bird. He had puffed his feathers out to look big and scary. The smaller bird knew he was a phony and paid him no mind.

The Bible describes our enemy as a roaring lion. A lion that roars is not to be feared because he has given his presence away, allowing his prey time to escape. When we are in tune with God, we don't need to fear Satan's tactics. Compared to God he is all blackbird bluff. Let's pay him no mind!

How can you remain in tune with God?

Bridging the Gap

Faith is the confidence that what we hope for will actually happen;
it gives us assurance about things we cannot see.

HEBREWS 11:1 NLT

Do you ever feel like there is an enormous gap between what you know
to be true in God's Word and what you feel to be true? Our feelings
are so fickle. They fluctuate depending on our circumstances, much as
our moods change with the weather. The good news is that they don't
change facts. God promises strength, wisdom, peace, hope, direction,
comfort, forgiveness, courage, eternal life, and so much more. These are
unchangeable—they are written in stone.

How do we move from the tyranny of emotions to the confidence of
faith? We must determine to believe what God says instead of what our
emotions say, and then declare his promises aloud. Then we do it again
and again and again until faith rises and bridges the gap.

**How can you give your emotions to God
and remain confident in your faith?**

Dust

For He Himself knows our frame;
He is mindful that we are but dust.

PSALM 103:14 NASB

A story is told of a little boy who heard his pastor reading Psalm 103 from the pulpit. When he read verse fourteen, the boy leaned over to his mother and whispered, "Mommy, what is butt dust?" That aside, it is rather disconcerting to note that God refers to us as nothing more than dust. He says, "Our days on earth are like grass; like wildflowers, we bloom and die. The wind blows, and we are gone—as though we had never been here."

The truth is that we are incredibly important dust to God. Listen to the litany of all God has done for the millions of tiny specks on this earth. He has forgiven our sins, rescued us from punishment, healed our diseases, filled our life with good things, and given us his righteousness. Merely dirt? Well, he knows our frame, because he framed us! He knows we are weak and mortal and without his powerful hand upon us, we would be irrecoverably destroyed.

How can you find your significance in God today?

Clay Pots

You, Lord, are our Father.
We are the clay, you are the potter;
we are all the work of your hand.

ISAIAH 64:8 NIV

There are many types of pottery—from basic earthenware used for mundane tasks to lovely, decorative pieces that adorn someone's mantelpiece. It is interesting to note that God uses this imagery all the way from Genesis to Revelation. He is the artist (potter); we are the clay. The potter has absolute power to create exactly according to his wish; the pot has no say.

There are times when we are not happy with the vessel the potter has fashioned. We'd rather be the vase on the mantelpiece that is used to hold a beautiful bouquet. The truth is, the vessel itself is not what gives it worth—as beautiful as it may be. The value lies in the contents.

What beautiful contents are in your vessel?

EAT FOR LIFE

Man does not live by bread alone, but man lives by everything
that proceeds out of the mouth of the LORD.
DEUTERONOMY 8:3 NASB

It isn't often that we err on the side of eating too little! Hunger pangs,
boredom, anxiety, even depression can propel us to the refrigerator.
There is one kind of food that we can ingest without restraint—the meat
of the Word.

The Scriptures are our spiritual food: a veritable banquet laid out for our
enjoyment. The Word will nourish, guide, comfort, convict, keep us from
sinning, and satisfy every hungry, thirsty soul. Read it and remember that
as one weakens physically without regular meals, so the soul will become
impoverished without habitual intake of the Word. Eat for life!

What nourishment can you take from the Scriptures today?

NECESSARY INSTRUMENT

All Scripture is inspired by God and profitable for teaching, for reproof, for correction, for training in righteousness; so that the man of God may be adequate, equipped for every good work.

2 TIMOTHY 3:16-17 NASB

Most tasks require a tool. In daily living it may be a broom, drill, lawnmower, hose, bucket, hammer, or parachute! It takes something to accomplish something.

In our spiritual lives we need tools as well. God never intended us to struggle along without the necessary instruments for success. Scripture, breathed by God, is the divine workshop complete with resources for the taking. Its purpose is to teach, correct, and convict so that we can live wisely! Are we reading, studying, and hiding the words in our hearts, or are we empty, dry, and ill-equipped for the life he has called us to? Open the Bible and ask God to help you implement the truths found there.

What instruments do you need for success?

FAITH'S END

"If you have faith like a grain of mustard seed, you will say to this mountain, 'Move from here to there,' and it will move, and nothing will be impossible for you."

MATTHEW 17:20 ESV

A teacher is about to illustrate the meaning of faith. He instructs a child to stand with his back toward him, close his eyes and fall backwards into his outstretched arms. The child needs a great measure of faith in that teacher. Is he trustworthy? Squeezing his eyes shut, the child falls backwards and is caught by the teacher who then explains how we similarly need to completely trust God.

Trusting God with no restraint is not always easy. It means we are at peace with whatever the outcome may be. Often we pray earnestly for a specific answer and we think that the outcome of that prayer reveals the measure of our faith. We long for healing, provision, a job, that miracle. But the end result of our faith is none of those things—it's the salvation of our souls! Don't over analyze your amount of faith. Stay in the Word and your faith will grow. In the meantime, fall into God's arms; he will catch you!

Do you trust God to catch you when you fall into him? Why or why not?

Held Together

He is before all things, and in him all things hold together.
COLOSSIANS 1:17 NIV

Often life seems to be a conglomeration of unrelated activities and we feel pulled in a thousand directions simultaneously. Loose ends, unfinished business, and to-do lists leave us feeling a day late and a dollar short. Frustration, discouragement, and anxiety often overwhelm. The apostle Paul must have experienced something similar when he was on a ship headed to Jerusalem to be tried in court. An enormous storm raged. In an effort to survive, the sailors wrapped ropes around the body of the ship to keep it from falling apart. God promised Paul that all would survive the wreck, and they did.

What an amazing truth it is to know that it is not our job to hold our lives together. Our responsibility is to submit our to-do list to God, bow to his will and let him hold it all together. He is the rope that holds us fast.

What is on your to-do list today?

THIS IS LOVE

This is love: that we walk in obedience to his commands. As you have heard from the beginning, his command is that you walk in love.

2 JOHN 6 NIV

Love is probably the most overused, over romanticized word in the human language. We fall in love, we love pizza, and we love our pet cat. Scripture tells us that we are supposed to love God. How do we love an invisible being?

In 1 John 2:3-5, John defines love for God by saying that the proof of our love for him is our obedience. We don't need to search for an elusive emotion. We just need to obey.

How can you be obedient to God today?

IDOLS OF THE HEART

Son of man, these leaders have set up idols in their hearts. They have embraced things that will make them fall into sin. Why should I listen to their requests?

EZEKIEL 14:3 NLT

God had a strong message for Israel. He told Ezekiel that he would not entertain the people's requests because they had set up idols in their hearts, which separated them from him. He wasn't talking about physical objects, but something of a different dimension. What did he mean? Possessions, prestige, position, power? Self, entertainment, rules, religion? Internet, sports, hobbies? Whatever consumes our time could become an idol of the heart.

Maybe it's time do to some soul searching. What squanders our time, our thoughts, and dictates our priorities? Are we embracing things that will lead us into sin? At times we wonder why God doesn't seem to be listening to our prayers. It's possible that there's an idol in the way.

What takes up most of your time?

Constant Joy

> Do not grieve, for the joy of the LORD is your strength.
> NEHEMIAH 8:10 NIV

Joy is not necessarily happiness. Happiness is dependent on circumstances; joy is not. Happiness is fleeting; joy is constant. Happiness disappears when trials come; joy grows through troubles. Good times bring happiness and laughter; difficulties bring sorrow and grief, but joy resides beneath.

Joy is not an emotion that can be fabricated or faked. It is a deep-seated sense that all things are well because God is in charge. Joy is expressed in praise, song, laughter, a peaceful countenance, a light in the eyes, or a serenity that belies any adversity. It is the substance of the soul that holds us together as we trust in God, who does all things well. Jesus wants our joy to be full!

What brings you the greatest joy?

KEPT

We know that anyone born of God does not continue to sin;
the One who was born of God keeps them safe,
and the evil one cannot harm them.

1 JOHN 5:1 NIV

Little Peter's legs are pumping as he heads toward the road. Mom yells, "Stop, stop!" If he is an obedient child, he will immediately put on the brakes. She protects him from danger, but his safety depends on his compliance.

In a similar way, God's Word is clear about what he expects of us. His purpose is to keep us from harm. If we have submitted ourselves to God, we will obey. However, God's involvement with our obedience is profound. He not only gives us the strength but the will to obey him, and then he goes a step further. He keeps us! God protects us from the evil that surrounds us and the sin we could easily fall into. This does not mean we will never be tempted, suffer, or go through hardship. It simply means we can persevere, kept by God's power.

How can you be more compliant to God's commands?
Do you see that they are put there to protect you?

END OF THE TUNNEL

> "I am the light of the world. Whoever follows me will never walk in darkness, but will have the light of life."
>
> JOHN 8:12 NIV

There's an old adage dating back to the 1800s we've probably all quoted: "There is a light at the end of the tunnel." Translated: "Hang on. The end of whatever difficulty you are in is in sight!" However, there are times when there probably is no positive ending to be had, and there is no light at the end of our tunnel. What then?

Jesus is light and he dwells in us. We are surrounded by his presence no matter where we are. He is behind us, before us, to the right and the left, above and beneath. We are cocooned in his presence and do not walk in darkness. He is our light. No more walking through dark tunnels with only a spot of hope at the end. We walk through our tunnels blazing with the light of Jesus!

Can you see the light at the end of the tunnel in your current circumstance?

Never Give Up

I call on you, my God, for you will answer me;
turn your ear to me and hear my prayer.

PSALM 17:6 NIV

Jesus taught that we should pray and never give up. He told of a widow who was being mistreated by an enemy and came to a judge hoping for a settlement. The judge, who didn't care about God or people, finally relented and reluctantly handed down a decision. Why? Because the widow approached him again and again and again.

God will never put us off or turn us away but will respond quickly. Our quickly may not be the same as God's though. Many times he waits to answer for a variety of reasons. Perhaps the most important reason is that in the waiting, we will learn to seek God, to keep crying out to him and trusting him against all odds. But pray we must. And then pray some more.

What have you been praying for that you need to persevere in?

PERENNIALS

As the soil makes the sprout come up
and a garden causes seeds to grow,
so the Sovereign LORD will make righteousness
and praise spring up before all nations.

ISAIAH 61:11 NIV

Jesus loved to tell stories about farmers and fields. We are familiar with his teaching on the seeds, the weeds, the pruning. Have you ever considered the perennial plant? It courageously weathers the winters and returns to grow and bloom. Some are garden bullies—they can rush over another plant without so much as an "excuse me." If you're not careful, your entire garden can be overrun by one aggressive plant.

In our lives, there are things that in themselves are not wrong. But when they are allowed to take over, they become a huge detriment to our spiritual growth. How much time do we spend on useless activities—computer games, Facebook, talk shows, television, movies? Maybe it's time to reign in the perennials in our lives, remembering our time on this earth is limited.

What, if anything, has been causing your spiritual growth to suffer?

Sins of Omission

To one who knows the right thing to do and does not do it,
to him it is sin.

JAMES 4:17 NASB

A young mom and her kids would often bike past an older lady resting in a chair in front of a shabby looking mobile home. Something stirred in the mom's heart, and she knew the woman needed the Gospel. She fully intended to stop by for a visit. Procrastination won out until it was too late. One day the woman's lot was completely empty… there was no sign of life and only a patch on the ground where the home had been.

Sins of commission are fairly obvious; those of omission are easier to rationalize away. The Holy Spirit prompts us to share Christ, or cut off a relationship, or invite the neighbor for dinner, but we're too harried, too consumed by our own plans. In our hearts, we know what we are to do, but somehow the commitment to obey is not there. Let's change that. Let's heed the gentle voice of the Holy Spirit.

**Can you think of any sins of omission in your life
that you want to hand over to God?**

Starting Over

Praise the LORD!
Oh, give thanks to the LORD, for He is good!
For His mercy endures forever.

PSALM 106:1 NKJV

Have you ever wished you could have a do-over? It would be so great to turn back the clock, reverse a decision, and do it differently. There is so much more wisdom in looking back. Yes, there are some things we can do over, like tweak the recipe or rip the seam, but most often, the important big decisions can't be changed.

Except when it comes to spiritual things. God tells us that we can start over every morning because his mercies will be there. Whatever went awry the day before, whatever mess we made from poor choices, we can begin the next day with a completely clean slate. There does not need to be any carryover of yesterday's mistakes. Our part in the transaction may require repentance of sin or forgiving someone, perhaps even ourselves. Bathed in his mercies, we can begin each day squeaky clean.

What does starting over look like to you?

DELIVERANCE TRILOGY

He has delivered us from such a deadly peril, and he will deliver us again. On him we have set our hope that he will continue to deliver us.

2 CORINTHIANS 1:10 NIV

Deliverance. What a marvelous word. It is liberation, emancipation, freedom, rescue. Anyone who has experienced the antonyms of any of these words knows the exhilaration of deliverance. Think of the demon-possessed man Jesus saved. Homeless, naked, living in a cemetery. He was guarded, shackled, chained, and completely controlled by an evil spirit. At Jesus' word, he was set free!

We, too, are in need of deliverance. Bound by sin and needing a Savior, we were delivered. When we battle temptation and confusion and our faith falters, we need to be delivered again. As adversity finds its way to our doorstep and difficulties overwhelm, we have the hope that God will continue to deliver us: past, present, and future.

What have you seen God deliver you from lately?

DiVINE SONG

Shout with joy to the LORD, all the earth;
burst into songs and make music.
Make music to the LORD with harps,
with harps and the sound of singing.
Blow the trumpets and the sheep's horns;
shout for joy to the LORD the King.

PSALM 98:4-6 NCV

The gift of music is surely from the heart of God to his creation. Melodies, harmonies, rhythms, and the infinite configuration of notes and styles inspire, soothe, and stimulate according to their genre. Mortal music is a wonder. Can you imagine the incredible beauty of heavenly instruments?

Keep the beauty of heavenly song in your mind, and then contemplate the fact that God surrounds us with songs of deliverance and even sings over us with melodies of victory. The purpose of this music is to hide us in his love, protect us from trouble, calm our fears, and give us the victory over the enemy. We are cocooned in the divine song. Let's sing our joyful praise back to God, for he is worthy.

What do you think heavenly instruments sound like?

THE VINE

"I am the vine, you are the branches; he who abides in Me and I in him,
he bears much fruit, for apart from Me you can do nothing."

JOHN 15:5 NASB

A mother often has a difficult time letting her children grow up and fly
the nest. She has given so much of herself, her time, and her energy to
their raising that their absence leaves a hollow place—a gaping hole. In
the serving, she has found fulfillment, nourishment, and meaning. Her
fountainhead of joy and life seems to have been sealed off.

This dilemma begs an explanation, and Jesus does it well in this verse.
He reminds us that he is the vine. We are the branches that must remain
in the vine in order to receive sustenance. If we are attached to anything
other than him—children, spouse, job, ministry—we will wither away
and die because those resources are merely human. We must stay
connected to Jesus. Without the life of the vine flowing through us, we
will bear no fruit.

**How can you gain a sense of worth and accomplishment
that comes from God alone?**

Three Things

We know that we belong to God, but the Evil One controls the whole world. We also know that the Son of God has come and has given us understanding so that we can know the True One. And our lives are in the True One and in his Son, Jesus Christ. He is the true God and the eternal life.

1 JOHN 5:19-20 NCV

We live in a world where absolutes seem to be a thing of the past. Many in our culture believe there are no absolutes because of the variables of background, ethnicity, and religion. Unfortunately, there are people in our churches who vacillate, succumbing to the influences of society. Grey areas have emerged where black and white should be.

John clearly states that we can know absolute truth. We know that God keeps us safe from sin and the evil one, we know we belong to God, and we can know the True One. It's all right there in God's Word.

What is absolute truth?

UNCHANGING

Jesus Christ is the same yesterday and today and forever.
HEBREWS 13:8 NASB

You may have heard the saying, "There is nothing permanent except change." The word change itself can evoke a number of responses: fear, dread, worry, sadness, or loss. It can produce a grief of sorts as we realize things will never be the same. There is safety in the familiar: a sense of continuity with the flow of life that is unsettling when altered.

Relationships change, friends move, loved ones pass on, culture shifts, aging takes place, and it can be painful. God knows this. He makes sure his Word contains the one assurance we are desperate to know. He never changes. He doesn't get old, or move away, or busy himself elsewhere. He is the same God who created the world, sent his Son to redeem us from our sin, and gave his Holy Spirit to be with us always. No matter how our lives change from day to day, we can bank on his constancy.

What changes have been difficult for you this year?

Waiting

Wait for the Lord;
Be strong, and let your heart take courage;
Yes, wait for the Lord!
PSALM 27:14 NASB

Is there anything positive to be said about waiting? Whether we are in line at the grocery store, stuck in traffic, or simply waiting for a package to arrive, it is part of our daily lives. Waiting seems like a colossal waste of time. And yet, God tells us specifically (35 times or so) we are to "wait for the Lord."

The concept of waiting on God seems to originate with the Psalmist. Perhaps it was because he was so often stuck in perilous situations and he knew his only hope was God. The kind of waiting he speaks of is not passive as though our spiritual lives are put on hold until God comes through with our request. It is an active display of faith as we lay down our desires, hopes, and dreams before the Lord and surrender to his will. In the waiting, he is perfecting our faith and building our character.

In what situation do you need to be patient and wait for God's timing?

WEAK STRENGTH

"My grace is sufficient for you,
for my power is made perfect in weakness."
Therefore I will boast all the more gladly about my weaknesses,
so that Christ's power may rest on me.

2 CORINTHIANS 12:9 NIV

There's something inside of us that longs to be strong and self-sufficient. Don't we admire the woman who can raise children, work, volunteer, and yet appear put together? Even if people like that don't really exist, in our minds they do! We get impatient with our weakness and insufficiencies.

What a relief to know that God doesn't expect us to be strong. In fact, the apostle Paul said he delighted in his weaknesses, insults, hardships, persecution, and difficulties. God isn't looking for us to be strong. He's looking for us to turn to him in our weaknesses so his power can rest upon us! Let's start being grateful for our shortcomings and give God a chance to demonstrate his power.

How can you allow God to demonstrate his power in your life?

Eye contact

Let your eyes look straight ahead;
fix your gaze directly before you.

PROVERBS 4:25 NIV

A stylish young lady is strolling along leisurely, texting with her friend. She glances up periodically to assess her location and then returns her gaze to the contraption she is holding. She senses a shadow looming and lifts her eyes, finding herself face-to-bark with a birch tree!

Keeping our spiritual eyes focused on what's ahead is even more important. Often we look around, searching for other resources to meet our needs, to solve our problems, to give us direction instead of looking straight to Jesus. The amazing truth is that God is longing to make eye contact with us. We look to Jesus, he looks back, and when our eyes meet—we have indeed touched the divine.

What image do you see when you picture God?

WILLING TO LEARN

Similarly, teach the older women to live in a way that honors God.
These older women must train the younger women to love their
husbands and their children, to live wisely and be pure, to work in their
homes, to do good, and to be submissive to their husbands.

TITUS 2:3-5 NLT

Mothers and daughters have a complex relationship that gradually shifts until they become peers. Ahead of the daughter by years of experience, the mother has much to give. However, the daughter may pass through a season where she is not interested in any wisdom from mom and is unwilling to learn. And yet, here the apostle Paul writes that older women should teach the younger ones to live a godly life.

This admonition is two-fold and potentially problematic. First, the older women must live circumspectly before the Lord and then be willing to teach others. Secondly, the younger women must be willing to learn! Sometimes the youthful prefer to learn from their peer group, viewing the elders as somewhat outdated. Conversely, the older woman may feel disconnected and extinct herself. Let's overcome these hindrances and be women who are willing to teach and willing to learn!

Who are you willing to teach? Who are you willing to learn from?

Complete Believer

When the way is rough, your patience has a chance to grow. So let it grow, and don't try to squirm out of your problems. For when your patience is finally in full bloom, then you will be ready for anything, strong in character, full and complete.

JAMES 1:3-4 TLB

We all will see our fair share of hard times in this life. In the difficulties, we will develop and grow into believers that are complete—ready for anything.

God has a heavenly, eternal perspective and he is shaping us and preparing us for things that are greater than what we can imagine. If we will hold on and trust him, he will reveal to us a more beautiful purpose than we could have dreamed.

How can you surrender yourself to God's process?

Helped

I will instruct you and teach you in the way you should go;
I will counsel you with my loving eye on you.

PSALM 32:8 NIV

Every day we are faced with fear, but sometimes fear becomes so great it starts to control us. What if, instead of being paralyzed by our fears, we told God what we were afraid of? God promises that he will hold our hand, calm our fears, and help us through whatever we're facing.

We don't have to walk alone in fear—we can be strengthened by God's truth and helped by his power.

How can you invite God into your fear-filled situations?

Songs of Victory

You are my hiding place;
you protect me from trouble.
You surround me with songs of victory.

PSALM 32:7 NLT

Life can feel like a battle sometimes. From keeping up with busy schedules to making major decisions, we are met with challenges daily. Some days we just want to hide away for a while so we can recharge and refocus.

God is our hiding place—our protection and our rest. He walks with us through the battles of life and sings a song of victory over us. With Christ as our strength, we can not only make it through the battle, we can come out as joyful victors.

What do you need God to help give you victory in today?

QUESTIONING SOUL

Trust in him at all times, you people;
pour out your hearts to him,
for God is our refuge.

PSALM 62:8 NIV

There are questions that we long to have answered by God, and circumstances in our lives that leave us wondering about his goodness. As we pray, we try to rend the heavens for an answer that will make sense of our storm.

What God desires most isn't the soul with the answer—it's the one laid bare before him in a perfect dance of trust, belief, and raw vulnerability. In that moment of emptiness before your Maker, he will be your safe place. Pour out your heart to him and rest in his embrace because he is a refuge for even the most questioning soul.

What deep questions are you looking for answers about?

Tested Promises

Your promises have been thoroughly tested,
and your servant loves them.
My eyes stay open through the watches of the night,
that I may meditate on your promises.
PSALM 119:140, 148 NIV

What has God promised you? Have you felt his promise through a certain Scripture? Or perhaps through words spoken over your life that cast a vision in your soul? When God promises something, it takes faith to believe that he will bring it to pass.

Years may go by from the moment of vision to the moment of fruition. The waiting can either be a time of bitterness, or it can be a time of great sweetness with the Lord as you grow in trust, faith, and praise.

What dreams do you have for your future?

FOR US

What, then, shall we say in response to these things?
If God is for us, who can be against us?

ROMANS 8:31 NIV

God is for us. What a powerful idea that the God of the universe is for us. We sometimes buy into this untruthful image of God, depicting him as angry, distant, and condemning. But God is for us; he is not against us. His heart toward us has eternally been compassionate, loving, merciful, and tender.

God's desire for unhindered relationship with us is displayed impeccably by Christ—who laid everything down to fight for our hearts.

What do you need God to be "for you" in today?

COMFORT

Praise be to the God and Father of our Lord Jesus Christ, the Father of compassion and the God of all comfort, who comforts us in all our troubles, so that we can comfort those in any trouble with the comfort we ourselves receive from God.

2 CORINTHIANS 1:3-4 NIV

When we face trouble, God doesn't just watch us struggling from a distance. He is our comfort, our strength, and our hope. And as he comforts us, he also teaches us how to comfort others.

Whatever difficult thing we may have walked through, there is someone else who is walking through something very, very similar. Our experiences can be the one thing that keeps that person afloat during their hard time.

Who can you offer comfort to today?

Encouraged in Faith

*When we get together, I want to encourage you in your faith,
but I also want to be encouraged by yours.*

ROMANS 1:12 NLT

True, life giving friendship will be characterized by a mutual encouragement of faith in Christ. Have you ever had a friend who, after you've been with them, makes you want to know God more? A friend whose love for the Lord is infectious? That is the type of friendship that we should strive to surround ourselves with: the kind of friend who will point us to Christ and make us long for his presence.

True friendship results in true fellowship—a source of strength, community, and accountability.

Which friends encourage and strengthen you? Thank God for them today.

STRONGHOLD

The LORD is good,
A stronghold in the day of trouble;
And He knows those who trust in Him.

NAHUM 1:7 NKJV

God isn't only with us when our faith comes easy and our praise is unrestrained. Even in the day of trouble, God knows intimately those who trust him, and he is a stronghold for them.

Not only in catastrophe, but even in our moments of hidden weakness, God is our strength and our refuge. We can trust him and know that he is always good.

What do you need to trust God with today?

Power of seeking

Even there you can look for the LORD your God,
and you will find him if you look for him with your whole being.

DEUTERONOMY 4:29 NCV

Do you have days when you feel empty, weary, and uninspired? Days when you feel you have nothing to give, even though there is no shortage of demand. You don't know how to fill back up; you only know that you need to.

The Lord says that if you look for him with your whole being, you will find him. God will not withhold himself from his child who asks. Even here, in this place of emptiness, you can be filled—you just have to seek.

**Write a prayer asking God to meet with you
in the deepest place of your heart.**

ALTAR OF SACRIFICE

> While God was testing him, Abraham still trusted in God and his promises, and so he offered up his son Isaac and was ready to slay him on the altar of sacrifice.
>
> HEBREWS 11:17 TLB

Have you ever received a promise from God only to then be led to relinquish it? Isaac was Abraham's son of promise—a dream given by God, granted—now demanded in offering.

Why would God give us vision and promise and then ask for us to lay that same dream down on the altar? Perhaps it's because it's only in the crucifixion that we find the resurrection. In the laying down and the dying that we find the abundant life of salvation.

What is God asking you to do that seems impossible right now?

STRENGTH

It is God who arms me with strength
and keeps my way secure.
He makes my feet like the feet of a deer;
he causes me to stand on the heights.
He trains my hands for battle;
my arms can bend a bow of bronze.

PSALM 18:32-34 NIV

God may require us to do something that we don't feel equipped for, but he will always give us what we need to accomplish it. We may wonder if he chose the wrong person, or if we didn't hear his call correctly, but God can enable us to take on any task necessary to further his kingdom.

When God gives us something to do, or somewhere to be, we can rest assured that he will train and equip us fully in order to accomplish it.

What faults do you think are stopping you from doing what God is asking? Can you give those to God and let him be your strength?

Worthy

"You are worthy, O Lord,
To receive glory and honor and power;
For You created all things,
And by Your will they exist and were created."

REVELATION 4:11 NKJV

Worship is our natural response to the goodness of God. It's not simply an emotional reaction—worship is also the act of offering back to God the glory that he rightly deserves. When we stop to think about God's power, majesty, and creativity, we cannot help but glorify him because he is so worthy of the highest form of honor.

By glorifying God in our daily lives, those around us will take notice and some will ultimately be led to join us in praising him.

Write a song of praise to God for all he has done.

RETURN

"If you return to the LORD, your brothers and your sons will find compassion before those who led them captive and will return to this land. For the LORD your God is gracious and compassionate, and will not turn His face away from you if you return to Him."

2 CHRONICLES 30:9 NASB

When we have sin in our life, it can be tempting to run from God and hide. We don't want him to see our weakness, and we fear his judgment. Our sin creates a barrier in our hearts between ourselves and God. It blinds us to his mercy and grace.

Covered in shame, we are without the confidence of a child living in freedom. But the Lord beckons us to return to him, promising compassion, grace, and restored favor.

How have you found the Lord's compassion in your moments of weakness?

WHO I AM

He continued by questioning them, "But who do you say that I am?"
Peter answered and said to Him, "You are the Christ."

MARK 8:29 NASB

We must determine who we say Jesus is. Even Peter, who had walked closely with Jesus, was still asked this potent question: "Who do you say I am?" We can follow Jesus, walk with him, even be a devout follower, but who do we truly believe he is in our hearts?

Our belief about who Jesus is has a direct impact on our relationship with him. Do we believe he is our salvation and our only hope? Jesus' identity cannot change no matter who you believe him to be: he is the Messiah, the son of God—undeniably. But who you say and believe Jesus is will make all the difference in your heart.

Who do you believe God to be?

EYES WILL SEE

Your eyes will see the King in His beauty;
They will behold a far-distant land.
ISAIAH 33:17 NASB

On the difficult days when our faith is weak, our tears flow freely, and our hearts are discouraged, we wish just to see God. We think that if we could look into his eyes, have the chance to ask him our deepest questions—and hear them answered—then we could continue on.

Beloved, the reality of heaven is closer than we can imagine. We will see our King, in all his greatness and his beauty. We will look upon that distant land of heaven. We will one day dwell there in peace: with every question answered and every tear dried.

What do you imagine when you think of heaven?

Ruled by Emotion

Then we will no longer be immature like children. We won't be tossed and blown about by every wind of new teaching. We will not be influenced when people try to trick us with lies so clever they sound like the truth.

EPHESIANS 4:14 NLT

God has called us to be overcomers. He desires for us to stand firm in what we know to be true, rather than to be ruled by our varying emotions. As we mature in Christ, the truth of God's Word will come to carry more weight in our hearts than our own feelings do.

Feelings are important to acknowledge and validate. When we submit them to God, we will find growth, maturity, and strength to remain strong in the faith while still allowing our emotions to have their rightful place.

Do you feel like you are at the mercy of your emotions?
How can you surrender them to God without invalidating how you feel?

Unhindered

Because of Christ and our faith in him,
we can now come boldly and confidently into God's presence.
EPHESIANS 3:12 NLT

Our salvation awards us the great privilege of being able to approach God unhindered. With sin no longer dividing us from his holy presence, we are free to bare our souls to God as his beloved sons and daughters.

As bold and confident lovers of God, there is nothing we cannot share with him—and he with us. Fear and shame have no place in this kind of excellent love.

What shame do you need God to take away from you today?

Focus

I have set the LORD continually before me;
Because He is at my right hand, I will not be shaken.
PSALM 16:8 NASB

The mark of a purposeful life is strong focus. When we fix our eyes on a goal, we are far less likely to become distracted by conflicting interests. By setting the Lord continually before us, we become fixated on the greatest possible purpose.

This resolution of focus steadies us; we cannot be shaken, deterred, or destroyed while we are so firmly positioned toward Christ. There are few things more powerful than Christians who have determined to allow nothing to hinder them from achieving God's purposes and plans.

What are you doing to achieve your top goals?
Are they in line with God's will?

Fulfilling Dreams

Only let each person lead the life that the Lord has assigned to him,
and to which God has called him. This is my rule in all the churches.

1 CORINTHIANS 7:17 ESV

God created you perfectly to be the person he planned for you to be. He
has plans for your life and purposes for your talents. When we long to be
someone else, or somewhere else, we miss out on the incredible plan that
God has for who we are right where we are.

By devoting ourselves to live the life we've been called to, we fulfill God's
excellent dream for our lives. There is no greater privilege than to honor
our creator by living out the purpose he planned for us.

What dreams do you believe God has given you?

In a Desert

He found them in a desert,
a windy, empty land.
He surrounded them and brought them up,
guarding them as those he loved very much.

DEUTERONOMY 32:10 NCV

Do you ever go through seasons in your life where you just feel dark? Perhaps directionless or uninspired? In a metaphorical wilderness where you can't get a glimpse of any vision or even hope, God can find you. Even in the deserts of your own heart where you can't muster the strength to reach out to him, he can and will meet you.

Wait for the Lord, even in your emptiness; wait for him and he will come for you.

What seasons in life have felt dark and uninspired? Do you believe that God can find you even in the middle of those dark seasons?

GOD OF COMPASSION

The LORD is good to everyone.
He showers compassion on all his creation.
PSALM 145:9 NLT

The good things in your life—material, internal, spiritual, or social—are expressions of God's regard for you. When God looks upon you, his heart fills with compassion… and he is always looking upon you.

God comforts and heals you when you are broken and hurting. He doesn't have a hot temper, he never breaks any of his promises, and he always does the right thing. Moreover, if you honestly call on him, he runs to your side.

What desires are you asking God to grant you?

DEATH TO LIFE

God, being rich in mercy, because of His great love with which He
loved us, even when we were dead in our transgressions, made us alive
together with Christ.

EPHESIANS 2:4 NASB

Every autumn, summer's deep green leaves fade into a thousand shades
of gold and red. Their fiery beauty lasts for a few weeks but eventually
browns and falls to the ground under the weight of the wind. Trees
shake barren in the cold, already anticipating spring and the buds which
will once again decorate empty branches.

A simple, yet seemingly harsh, law of generation: there must be death for
there to be new life. Mirrored by creation, we all have things in our lives
which need to die in order for new life to be breathed on us. Old habits,
negative relationships, damaging thoughts—whatever must die so that the
new life in Christ can grow is well worth the exchange.

**What old habits, negative relationships, or damaging thoughts do you
need to turn over to God today?**

END OF DEATH

He will swallow up death forever. The Sovereign LORD will wipe away
the tears from all faces; he will remove his people's disgrace from all
the earth.

ISAIAH 25:8 NIV

How beautiful it is to think that all we fear and all we've been ashamed
of will someday be erased. Death, our ultimate enemy, will be swallowed
up completely when God has his eternal victory.

When we have put our hope in the Lord, we have the most incredible
promise ahead of us. Any temptation to despair or to become
overwhelmed with our present circumstances should disappear when
we remember the hope we have ahead. We are partakers in a hope that
knows no sorrow, children of a King who knows no defeat.

How does the promise of eternity help ease the curse of death?

THE FAILURE'S HEART

May our Lord Jesus Christ himself and God our Father, who loved us
and through grace gave us eternal comfort and good hope, comfort
your hearts and strengthen them in every good work and word.

2 THESSALONIANS 2:16-17 NRSV

God doesn't leave us alone in our weakness. When we feel incapable,
he gives us the strength we lack to accomplish the task. When we are
working sincerely for him, our work—no matter how insignificant it may
seem—will always be effective.

We may feel like a failure in the eyes of those around us, but in the eyes
of the Lord, our work done for his kingdom is never wasted. He cares
enough about our hearts to comfort us in times of failure, and to value us
in our moments of insignificance.

Do you feel like a failure? How can you begin to see yourself in God's eyes?

FATHER KNOWS BEST

This is the confidence we have in approaching God: that if we ask anything according to his will, he hears us. And if we know that he hears us—whatever we ask—we know that we have what we asked of him.

1 JOHN 5:14-15 NIV

Our prayers are not offered up to a silent heaven. When we pray, we are heard by a God who cares deeply about what we bring before him. By understanding the depth of his interest we gain confidence to approach him boldly in prayer.

God is a good Father who will not be swayed into giving us anything that is not to our benefit. We can present our requests to God freely knowing that if what we ask for is not what is best for our lives, then it will not be given to us.

What are you asking God for today?

Giant Obstacle

David said to the Philistine, "You come to me with sword and spear and javelin; but I come to you in the name of the LORD of hosts, the God of the armies of Israel, whom you have defied."

1 SAMUEL 17:45 NRSV

When young David met the champion Goliath in battle, he was so focused on the Lord that the giant who stood before him became nothing more than an obstacle to be overcome. Even when the voice of the giant taunted David, he was unaffected because his trust was securely placed in the almighty God.

We must let God overcome the giants of self-doubt that try to keep us bound in complacency.

What voices of negativity do you need to silence right now?

Kindness and Repentance

"Love your enemies, and do good, and lend, expecting nothing in return; and your reward will be great, and you will be sons of the Most High; for He Himself is kind to ungrateful and evil men."

LUKE 6:35 NASB

If kindness is what leads to repentance, then we must first be kind to the unrepentant. Throughout Scripture we see examples of the kindness and mercy of God toward those who don't deserve it. All of us, at one time, were ungrateful and evil—but God still pursued us with his excellent love regardless of our position. It was his unrelenting kindness that brought us to our knees.

We who have been forgiven of so much must testify of the grace we've been shown by extending it freely to those who still find themselves in darkness.

What kindnesses do you see God granting you in this season?

FILLING THE EMPTINESS

O God, you are my God; earnestly I seek you;
my soul thirsts for you;
my flesh faints for you,
as in a dry and weary land where there is no water.

PSALM 63:1 ESV

We all experience seasons where we feel emptiness: an ache deep within us that is inexplicable but present all at once. In those times, when we aren't sure what it is that we're longing for, it is more of God that we need.

Deep in the heart of every person, there is an innate need for intimacy with our creator. Without it our souls faint for want of him. But the beautiful truth is that he longs to fill us with himself. We have only to seek him in expectation.

What are you longing for?

Same Spirit

The Spirit of God, who raised Jesus from the dead, lives in you.
And just as God raised Christ Jesus from the dead, he will give life to
your mortal bodies by this same Spirit living within you.

ROMANS 8:11 NLT

The Spirit of revelation that reveals mysteries of eternity is the same Spirit that speaks to you. The Spirit of power that makes blind men see is the same Spirit that heals you. The Spirit that makes dead men live is the same Spirit that brings you to life.

As a believer, the Holy Spirit of God dwells within you and transforms every facet of your life.

**How does God enable you to live a life worthy of the calling
he has placed on you?**

Happy

The LORD will not forsake his people, for his great name's sake, because it has pleased the LORD to make you a people for himself.

1 SAMUEL 12:22 ESV

What could be more rewarding than to know that you please the Lord? When you enter into a relationship with God, he promises to never leave you. He's with you for the long haul, not only because it's not in his nature to leave, but also because—simply put—you make him happy.

Often we convince ourselves that we have disappointed God. This translates into shame in our relationship with him. But God is pleased with us, and he longs to speak that over us. Spend time today delighting yourself in the Lord, and feeling his delight over you in return.

How do you think you make God happy?

HOME CONSTRUCTION

"Everyone then who hears these words of mine and does them will be like a wise man who built his house on the rock. And the rain fell, and the floods came, and the winds blew and beat on that house, but it did not fall, because it had been founded on the rock."

MATTHEW 7:24-25 ESV

Every wise builder, regardless of what region of the world they come from, know the most important piece of building a home is the location of the foundation. That is why Jesus admonishes us to build on rock and not sand. In good weather, both locations might look sturdy. One might not see the inherent weakness of hard, dried sand.

But the earth doesn't stay hard and dry. Rains, floods, and winds come at their own whim, and this is when location matters the most. What looked strong at first quickly comes crashing down when the floor turns to sinking sand. The house on the rock is not immune to hardship, but it cannot be destroyed because it was built on the right foundation.

How can you build your house on the right foundation?

True Peace

"I leave you peace; my peace I give you. I do not give it to you as the world does. So don't let your hearts be troubled or afraid."

JOHN 14:27 NCV

For children, gifts tend to be the highlight of parties. As a child, you like having friends celebrate you, and eating cake drenched in copious amounts of frosting is fun, but the act of opening presents is the real joy of a birthday party. Perhaps this is sadly lost on adults. We age out of wanting gifts, thinking we are too old. Scripturally though, God seems to be the eager parent, anxiously waiting for his children to draw near to him so he can impart gifts. He loves to give.

Jesus is the only one able to give true peace, and he loves to give it to us. Receive today gifts from the Father that only he can give. He might not be giving you what you think you want, but he is giving you gifts that will sustain and satisfy your heart.

What situation do you need God's peace in today?

Stronger for Waiting

They who wait for the LORD shall renew their strength.

ISAIAH 40:31 ESV

Have you ever waited on someone? When you wait, you abdicate your ability to determine when something will happen. You are dependent on someone else.

When we wait on God, it can be incredibly difficult. Truly waiting on him means we aren't solving situations on our own. We wholly place our dependence and trust in God's solution, knowing it will be better than ours or anyone else's. Waiting is not natural. We would much prefer to act, even at the risk of acting incorrectly, than to wait on God. Even if we've waited a week or twenty years, his promise to us remains: if we persevere in waiting, we will become stronger.

What are you waiting for right now?

Collected Tears

You have seen me tossing and turning through the night. You have collected all my tears and preserved them in your bottle! You have recorded every one in your book.

PSALM 56:8 TLB

Our grief is near to God's heart. He longs to console us: to stroke our hair, wipe our tears, and whisper comfort. He counts the nights we toss and turn; he collects our tears. God isn't absent in our sorrow, rather the opposite—he is closer than ever.

Don't be afraid to come to God with your grief. Share with him the deepest feelings in your heart without holding back. In his presence you will find comfort, hope, compassion, and more love than you could imagine.

Are you in a season of grief?
How can you let God be your comforter in this time?

OUTWARDLY WASTING

We do not give up. Our physical body is becoming older and weaker,
but our spirit inside us is made new every day.

2 CORINTHIANS 4:16

Aging isn't a valued trait in much of the Western world. Entire industries
gross millions of dollars each year to help disguise age. Tell-tale signs
of aging like hair color and skin elasticity are not seen as a badge of
honor but something to hide. We don't even like to acknowledge our
age because it is virtuous to look younger than we actually are. Is this a
Biblical or worldly concept? Have you indulged in the lie that you have
been fed?

Ancient cultures, like the Hebrews, have a more Biblical view of aging.
Aging is honored because it means you have endured and persevered
longer than others. Often with age comes wisdom, and that is to be
admired. One thing we cannot do is stop the aging process. But with age
comes inward renewal and beauty for followers of God.

**What do you like about yourself more now than you did
when you were younger?**

Light and Momentary

Our light and momentary troubles are achieving for us
an eternal glory that far outweighs them all.
2 CORINTHIANS 4:17 NIV

Let's be honest, how many of us would be offended to have a dear friend tell us our troubles were light and momentary? Perhaps some troubles really are light and momentary; they only last for a few moments, and by night you hardly remember them. Maybe you ran out of gas on your way to the store, or you were late to a meeting. But have you buried someone you loved? Have you been abandoned by those you trusted? Can those troubles still be considered light and momentary?

Biblically speaking, they can. This is because all trouble in this life is considered light when compared to our eternal glory. If we can grasp that this age is temporary and will pass before we know it, then we will better be able to weather the troubles that happen here. When we step into the eternal, glorious age to come, we will confidently say that the glory we see there far outweighed every trouble experienced here.

**What light and momentary struggles don't feel that way at all?
Does viewing them in the light of eternity bring you hope?**

My Gift

Like good stewards of the manifold grace of God,
serve one another with whatever gift each of you has received.

1 PETER 4:10 NRSV

We most commonly think of a gift as something that is given to us for our own enjoyment and benefit. But in the kingdom of God, a gift is given to a person for the enjoyment and benefit of others. What could be more Christ-honoring than to give our gifts away so that others can be blessed?

If the church is to grow and be edified, then selfishness can have no place in it. Each time we use our own gifts to better others, we are retelling the gospel with our lives.

What gifts can you use to further God's kingdom?

HOPE OF GLORY

God decided to let his people know this rich and glorious secret which he has for all people. This secret is Christ himself, who is in you. He is our only hope for glory.

COLOSSIANS 1:27 NCV

Let's take a moment to contemplate true strength. Your body may feel weak to you on a day-to-day basis. But, if you are a child of God, you are not the only one indwelling your body. Christ is in you, and that is the hope of glory.

To walk in the knowledge and peace that Christ is in you, by his spirit, is abiding in a place of enormous strength. We know that Jesus is greater than anything and anyone. Acknowledge the powerful truth that if you are born again, Christ is dwelling in you. The same power that raised Jesus from the dead also rests in you—and that will be the power that raises you with him on the day he calls you to your eternal home. Indeed, this is the hope of glory.

What does "the hope of glory" mean to you?

REWARDS OR WRATH

"Store up for yourselves treasures in heaven, where neither moth nor
rust destroys, and where thieves do not break in or steal."
MATTHEW 6:20 NASB

In this life, you can, and do, make a direct impact on your life in the age
to come. The Bible teaches a lot on the principle of storing up various
things for the eternal age. When you store them, you don't see them now.
You set things aside, either consciously or unconsciously, to receive in
eternity. It is your retirement package for the age to come.

Stubborn people with unrepentant hearts actually store up wrath. This
shouldn't scare believers because they have approached God already in
humility and repentance. For believers there is much better news: they
are storing up rewards. Let's store up treasures that won't rust—to be
enjoyed for all eternity.

What treasures are you storing up for yourself in heaven?

No Longer Infants

This work must continue until we are all joined together in the same faith and in the same knowledge of the Son of God. We must become like a mature person, growing until we become like Christ and have his perfection.

EPHESIANS 4:13 NCV

When we first come to Christ, we are babies in the faith—regardless of our actual age. As God begins his work of making us like him, he feeds us gentle baby food. While infants are adorable, they aren't meant to stay that way. God matures us by his Spirit, feeding us food that we have to chew. This food is meaty and it satisfying, but we have to process it.

The passage in Ephesians 4 refers to our maturing through solid teaching of the Word of God. Many teachings of Jesus are simple to hear but hard to do. A mature child of God can receive and do what God asks without being offended. Infants aren't mature or grounded in the Word. They are susceptible to being tossed back and forth by poor teaching. Praise God that it is his work to mature us!

How have you matured spiritually in the past year?

MiND CONTROL

If people's thinking is controlled by the sinful self, there is death.
But if their thinking is controlled by the Spirit, there is life and peace.
ROMANS 8:6 NCV

Our minds are a powerful tool. No action takes place, whether good or bad, without starting first as a thought in the mind. Your mind dictates your entire body. What you give your thoughts to has direct implications on the actions you take. God calls us to be transformed by first renewing our minds so we will rightly discern his will.

But controlling and renewing our minds isn't natural to us. Often we feel helpless or subject to the thoughts that come through our brains, and we find ourselves entertaining them without even being conscious we are doing so. That is why God has given us the most necessary and precious gift—his Spirit. Apart from his Spirit, we are powerless to steward our thoughts well. When his Spirit controls our thoughts, we'll find that our minds move from anxiety, fear, and death to life and peace.

What places in your mind do you need to submit to Christ?

NOT SEPARATED

"Know therefore that the LORD your God is God; he is the faithful God, keeping his covenant of love to a thousand generations of those who love him and keep his commandments."

DEUTERONOMY 7:9 NIV

Has someone ceased to love you? What was the offense that put their love over the edge? Too many infractions? Too much broken trust? Your apology did not seem sincere? Maybe you have ceased to love someone. Human love is frail. This is why it is all the more critical not to put human attributes on God. His love is nothing like ours.

Enjoy your Father's steadfast love today. His love is incapable of failing you because nothing has the power to separate you from it. Don't berate yourself for your fickle love; be strengthened in his unfailing love.

How does it make you feel to know that you can never be separated from God's love?

Gift of Weakness

When Uzziah became powerful, his pride led to his ruin.
He was unfaithful to the Lord his God.

2 CHRONICLES 26:16 NCV

King Uzziah became King of Judah when he was 16 years old. 2 Chronicles 26 speaks highly of him as he began his young reign as king. He did what was right in the eyes of the Lord and as long as he sought the Lord, God gave him success. But something changed part way through his reign. His strength actually became his weakness. It led to pride and his ultimate destruction.

Have you ever considered that your weaknesses might be gifts from God? They might be what forces you into humility because you know that you aren't perfect and are always in need of a savior. God resists the proud, but the humble in heart can draw near to him. Which are you?

What areas of your life need a new level of humility?

TALKING BACK

> Who indeed are you, a human being, to argue with God?
> Will what is molded say to the one who molds it, "Why have you made
> me like this?"
>
> ROMANS 9:20 NRSV

Have you ever found yourself talking back to God? We do so when we think we know better, or when we think we see more clearly. We sometimes think our earthly wisdom exceeds that of our maker. We might talk back when we are sincerely hurting over tough—and sometimes tragic—circumstances.

It's not that God isn't thick-skinned enough to handle our questions. They don't rattle him or make him insecure. But often they don't help us an ounce. Spiritual maturity shows when you can whole-heartedly acknowledge to God that you don't understand but you still trust him. He is love. Everything he does is love. You can count on that.

Do you sometimes think you know better than God?
How can you submit those thoughts to him?

NOT THERE

"Where were you when I laid the foundation of the earth?
Tell me, if you have understanding."

JOB 38:4 NRSV

Have you been in a spiritual storm? Storms are painful because they expose our weakness and doubt before us and God—and sometimes others. Often God uses, and sometimes even creates, storms so that he can have our undivided attention.

God isn't being cruel to Job in his questioning. He is helping Job see that God is much bigger. If God was capable of orchestrating the intricate design of the earth, then surely he is capable of leading Job's life with the same care and wisdom. Even though it might look otherwise, God is to be trusted. Listen for his voice in your storm.

What would you love to understand about God?

Gift of Discipline

No discipline seems pleasant at the time, but painful. Later on,
however, it produces a harvest of righteousness and peace for those
who have been trained by it.

HEBREWS 12:11 NIV

We all appreciate well-disciplined children. Children that have learned, at some point, that they must submit to their parents are a delight to be around. While they are still fully children, they exhibit a humility that submits to rules and authority—even when they don't like it.

As children of God, we can also take comfort when he disciplines us. The heart of God in disciplining us is clearly that he does it in love, for our benefit. He is serious about dealing with sin in our hearts, and this will naturally be painful. But we should be encouraged; if we submit to the discipline of God in our lives, he gives us a precious gift—a harvest of righteousness and peace. Who doesn't want a more peaceful heart?

How do you feel you are being disciplined by God?

Running Free

Since we are surrounded by such a great cloud of witnesses, let us throw off everything that hinders and the sin that so easily entangles. And let us run with perseverance the race marked out for us.

HEBREWS 12:1 NIV

Have you ever watched a runner hindered by added baggage? In the Olympics, do you see runners racing with a backpack on their back? Hiking boots, jeans, coats, or sweatshirts? No. Trained runners run as leanly as they can. They wear aerodynamic shoes, sleeveless shirts, and thinly weighted shorts. Their goal is to not be hindered by anything so they might run the best possible race.

The author of Hebrews correlates our Christian pilgrimage to that of a runner in a race. We have the power to make our run much easier. The Holy Spirit is excellent at specifically showing us what is hindering us. We weren't designed to run a sluggish race—sin and disobedience cause that. Through the Spirit's power, you can throw off anything that hinders you and run.

What do you need to let go of so you can run without anything holding you back?

LOVE JUSTICE

Let the fear of the LORD be upon you. Judge carefully,
for with the LORD our God there is no injustice or partiality or bribery.

2 CHRONICLES 19:7 NIV

God had set up a system for Israel and Judah to manage themselves as a nation. Part of that system included setting apart judges who would rightly and wisely rule when there was a dispute. His call to the appointed judges was powerful. For a nation that was created to represent and be a blessing to the world, it was really important for them to have just judges. They represented God.

Do you long for justice in a specific area of your life? How about for the countless disenfranchised victims in the world? You must know that your passion for justice comes from God's heart. Not everything looks fair and equitable right now. But this isn't the end. Your just Judge will judge the world rightly when all is said and done. Even more mind-blowing is that he already judged us by pouring his wrath on Jesus on the cross, so none would have to pay the ultimate price for our sin.

What do you long for God to apply his justice to?

STORED GOODNESS

How abundant are the good things
that you have stored up for those who fear you,
that you bestow in the sight of all,
on those who take refuge in you.

PSALM 31:19 NIV

David, who enjoyed a great friendship with God, makes many wonderfully startling claims about God. God is storing up goodness. What exactly is that goodness? Is it safety and security? Is it peace in trials? Is it a quiet heart in the middle of a storm? Is it joy in the midst of mourning? Yes, it would seem that his goodness could be all of these and much more.

There is so much goodness that God actually has to store it, so he doesn't drench us in it all at once. But there is a caveat. The goodness referenced in this passage is reserved for a special group of people—those who fear God. It is for those who humbly come to him because he is the King and they are not. Rest assured, God will reward you more than your wildest dreams for loving him like that.

How do you see the goodness of God in your life?

LEARN FROM ME

*"Come to me, all you who are weary and burdened,
and I will give you rest."*
MATTHEW 11:28 NIV

Perhaps it's morning when you are reading this. Your day is just beginning, yet your heart is already heavy. Or maybe it's the end of the day and you feel weakened by the burdens you have taken on. Rest in the kindest person there ever was. Let his words soothe and strengthen you.

Perhaps you have taken on more than what God is asking you to—physically or emotionally. Christ himself makes it clear that his yoke is easy and his burden is light. If your yoke is too heavy, perhaps you aren't supposed to be carrying it in the first place. Learn from Jesus. Refusing wrong yokes won't necessarily feel natural to you. But ask and learn. As you do, he will strengthen your ability to know the difference, so you might enjoy his rest.

**Are the yokes in your life too heavy for you to bear?
What could you let go of?**

A FRIEND

> "I no longer call you servants, because a servant does not know his master's business. Instead, I have called you friends, for everything that I learned from my Father I have made known to you."
>
> JOHN 15:15 NIV

Pharisees knew the Law but rarely knew the spirit of the Law. There are many issues where they were passionate about obeying the Law, but their hearts were far from God. This is a dangerous place to be. God is far more interested in a humble and a contrite heart than cold-hearted obedience to his Law with a bitter spirit.

Have you ever found yourself obeying the commands of God but with a heart that was far from his? Be careful of this tendency. We can sometimes be rule-keepers without walking in deep friendship with God. God is not just looking for a servant; he is looking for a friend. Servants obey because they have to. Friends walk in close relationship because they understand shared love.

What do you enjoy about God's friendship?

Ask, seek, knock

"Ask and it will be given to you; seek and you will find; knock and the door will be opened to you. For everyone who asks receives; the one who seeks finds; and to the one who knocks, the door will be opened."

MATTHEW 7:7-8 NIV

Has your faith gotten weaker over time? Have some of your harder experiences left your more faithless than hopeful? Remember, regardless of the degree of your hard experiences, he promises to work everything out for good in your heart and life. Don't let your disappointments cloud the truth of God's Word. He promises that everyone who asks in his name receives.

Are you asking? Then you can count on receiving. Are you seeking? He promises you will find. Are you knocking? Yes, child, the door will be opened to you.

What are you asking, seeking, and knocking for today?

SELECTION

Be all the more diligent to make certain about His calling and choosing you; for as long as you practice these things, you will never stumble; for in this way the entrance into the eternal kingdom of our Lord and Savior Jesus Christ will be abundantly supplied to you.

2 PETER 1:10-11 NASB

Peter had just shared a crucial piece of wisdom for believers: when you have faith, be good. When you are good, be knowledgeable. When you are knowledgeable, be self-disciplined. When you are self-disciplined, become tenacious. When you are tenacious, become godly. When you are godly, become warm-hearted toward each other. When you are warm-hearted, become a lover. What a list!

Why did Peter continue to warn us that we should ensure we are called and chosen? Because to require a journey from faith to love is impossible, but to live and dwell in Christ makes for a fully satisfying, joy-filled journey. When you stumble, Jesus helps you up. When you are weak, he is strong. Assess your heart, and trust Jesus to it. Choose his blood for your power, grace, and mercy, and his presence as your constant companion. Stay in the journey fully dependent upon Jesus and all he is.

How can you choose Jesus today?

Discernment

See to it that no one takes you captive through philosophy and empty deception, according to the tradition of men, according to the elementary principles of the world, rather than according to Christ.

COLOSSIANS 2:8 NASB

The simplicity of the gospel can be offensive. This is because it relies solely on Jesus' complete work on the cross and not on our own merit. We are saved purely by receiving Christ's payment for our sins. He was able to pay for them fully because he provided a perfect sacrifice for the sins of all of mankind.

There are many false teachings that will try to lead you away from simple faith and trust in God's ability to save you. The responsibility to discern and not be taken captive by false teachings is on us. We have be rooted and grounded in the teachings of Jesus so that we can discern the difference between false teaching and the teachings of God. Let us build our faith wholly on Christ.

How can you ensure you are not being fooled by the world's doctrines and philosophies?

THE PROCESS

Put on your new nature, and be renewed as you learn
to know your Creator and become like him.
COLOSSIANS 3:10 NLT

While our salvation is a completed work, there is a continual working out of our faith. This is because God has called you into a relationship with himself. Relationships need to be nurtured and maintained. The word the Bible uses for this concept is renewal.

Even after salvation, our new self is still being renewed in knowledge in our creator's image. Our minds also need continual renewal. Don't be discouraged if you are still struggling with old ways of thinking or acting. Renewal is a process. Continue to repent and submit yourself to God. He is more passionate about renewing you than you are. He's a loving God who is committed to the process.

How can you renew your mind today?

IN ALL SITUATIONS

I have learned how to be content with whatever I have.
PHILIPPIANS 4:11 NLT

What an incredible gift Paul walked in. He knew how to be content regardless of how much or how little he had. It's interesting too that, as a believer, both situations arose in his life. There were times he had plenty and times he didn't. Did that mean God wasn't blessing him when he lacked? No, it simply meant those were the circumstances he found himself in. But you hear no accusatory overtone in Paul's writing here. He is not angry at God. He simply understood that following God would, or could, mean times of plenty and times of scarcity.

The secret to contentment is realizing that our circumstances don't determine our peace. We might be suffering or we might be on a mountaintop of victory, but our peace and our steadfast walk with God remain the same either way. Our joy is not contingent on our circumstance. Rather, we are satisfied that God will give us what we need when we need it.

What situation do you need to be content in right now?

STANDING BLAMELESS

To Him who is able to keep you from stumbling, and to make you stand in the presence of His glory blameless with great joy.

JUDE 1:24 NASB

Have you ever noticed what people did in Scripture when they were in the presence of an angel? Often they fell down, or they were so taken aback by the angel's presence that they had to be told not to fear. If that is what people do when they see angels, how do you suppose we will react upon seeing God himself? God calls us to stand before him. How will we even breathe?

Beloved, that we can stand blameless with great joy is an amazing truth that should cause us to arise with tears of gratitude. God does this for us because he no longer counts our sins against us. He has judged his Son in our place and has given us his Son's righteousness. We are blameless in his presence not because we don't sin, but because Jesus has paid for our sins.

How is it possible to stand blameless before God?

Confident Approach

Let us then approach God's throne of grace with confidence, so that we may receive mercy and find grace to help us in our time of need.

HEBREWS 4:16 NIV

Children were given parents so their basic needs could be met. It is a parent's job to provide food, shelter, and clothing. In a healthy home, if the children need anything else, they know they can go to their parents any time and make a request for what they need. This is especially true in crisis. If there is an urgent need, or a difficult situation, nothing delights a parent more than to see the child run to them to get help and wisdom.

That is a small picture of what God wants us to do with him. Are you in need? God invites you to confidently approach his throne. You need not be timid when you approach him; he says he will give you the mercy and grace you desperately need. Don't be afraid. You can confidently approach God in your hour of need.

Do you approach God with confidence? Why or why not?

Origin of Strength

"People do not live by bread alone,
but by every word that comes from the mouth of God."

MATTHEW 4:4 NLT

When Jesus was tempted by the devil, he had been in the wilderness fasting for forty days and forty nights. He wasn't consuming any calories during that time. Instead, he was giving all his energy to communing with the Father and being strengthened by their relationship. At the end of that time, Satan came to tempt him. Jesus withstood authentic temptation and never gave in.

It's interesting how God prepared Jesus for this trial. He didn't have him attend a conference, read a self-help book, or have a healing service. Instead, he led his son to be physically weaker so he could lean fully on the Father. Jesus had been on a 40-day diet of love, affirmation, and encouragement. He wasn't weakened by his lack of food. In fact, he made it clear that food alone wasn't what made a child of God strong. Perhaps that's one of the greatest gifts in fasting—we are able to see that it isn't food that sustains us but God's power in us.

Where do you find your strength?

LOVED FiRST

We love because he first loved us.

1 JOHN 4:19 NIV

Before Jesus began his earthly ministry, he was baptized by John the Baptist. John's job had been to prepare the way. Before Jesus was even on the public scene, he was calling people to repent. He would then baptize them. Jesus went to John to be baptized like many others, but he did this before he did anything else that was noteworthy. Yep, no miracles, no healings, and no deliverances are recorded from him prior to his baptism.

Immediately after he came up out of the water from his baptism, God spoke for all to hear: "This is my Son, whom I love; with him I am well pleased" (Matthew 3:17 NIV). What had Jesus done thus far? Nothing. He was simply God's son. Yet God's words to him were that of affirmation and love. Perhaps that's how God relates to us—his other children. He loves us because we are his. And we love him because he loved us. It's just that simple.

How does God's love for you help you to love others?

THE ETERNAL GIFT

"Give glory to God in heaven,
and on earth let there be peace among the people who please God."
LUKE 2:14 NCV

Christmas trees might be secular decorations, but they invoke, in Christians, thoughts of a more precious tree: the cross. Jesus came to us on Christmas day for the purpose of bringing peace to his people through the cross of Calvary.

Christ's mission was to redeem us from every thought, word, or action that didn't match up to our God-likeness. He destroyed our sins and silenced our enemy, permanently, on the cross. He empowered us for victory. Each of us carries his glory as a child of the Most High God. This is a Christmas gift for each of us to open every day.

How can you give glory to God today?

Executed Hope

"When you see the ark of the covenant of the Lord your God with the Levitical priests carrying it, then you shall set out from your place and go after it. Do not come near it, that you may know the way by which you shall go, for you have not passed this way before."

JOSHUA 3:3-4 NASB

Joshua stood at the cusp of the Promised Land. The Lord had spoken; the Israelites would consecrate themselves and then follow the Ark of the Presence into their promise. They would take God's new route to get there, so the vast camp traveled far behind the Ark, allowing each citizen to see it and faithfully follow God for themselves. In this manner, each Israelite successfully executed the actions of their faith before God rather than man. Led in the presence of God, every man crossed the Jordan, felled Jericho, and enjoyed the life of milk and honey promised him.

Today, each of us faces decisions that position us toward the fulfillment of God's promises in our lives. We take courage, consecrate ourselves, and follow him. Jesus has given us our land. We step into it, running the race with Jesus, and securing our hope. This day is our present opportunity.

What "land" are you being asked to step into today?

LOVE-JOY LIFE

"As the Father has loved me, so have I loved you. Abide in my love. If you keep my commandments, you will abide in my love, just as I have kept my Father's commandments and abide in his love. These things I have spoken to you, that my joy may be in you, and that your joy may be full."

JOHN 15:9-11 ESV

Joy comes into our lives through actions of obedience. Moreover, we may obey God for the sake of righteousness, but God rewards us for it by baptizing us in his love! As we abide in this love, we become vessels of joy, spilling onto dry places in the world around us. That joy will consume us, becoming a hallmark of his righteousness.

Strength and courage rise in the context of God's joy. We pursue and choose his ways, gaining fortitude to overcome, and we begin to live the supernatural life. In following the faithful one who overcame the world, we become like him, and we overcome as well.

How do you feel when you walk in obedience to God?

WATER OF LiFE

"Whoever drinks of the water that I shall give him will never thirst. But the water that I shall give him will become in him a fountain of water springing up into everlasting life."

JOHN 4:14 NKJV

Sometimes, we need extra. Our spiritual requirements are never met by earthly experiences. When these experiences occlude our spiritual opportunities, we leave off from them, thirsting. Life as expected derails—whether from internal failures or external events—and this creates great inner struggle. The verve inside us may dwindle in the face of such difficult challenges. Where will we get joy and strength to continue?

Jesus says he brings us abundant life wherever the enemy has tried to kill, steal, or destroy. He is just that faithful. His living water is an endless fountain. We reach up to him, relying upon him to fill us with this eternal life.

What "extra" do you need today?

FALSE EXPECTATIONS

This is how we know what love is: Jesus Christ laid down his life for us.
And we ought to lay down our lives for our brothers and sisters.

1 JOHN 3:16 NIV

Part of laying down one's life rests in relinquishing inappropriate expectations. When the highlight reel of your mind doesn't match your life, you hand that reel to Jesus. He returns to you belonging and peace. These two blessings hinge upon your identity in him, not upon your attempts to achieve.

God places his desires within the hearts of his holy ones. When they are ignited, these desires produce good things: creativity, productivity, and charity toward others. You are not a failure. You are a possibility—God's possibility—opening up in the light of Jesus like a flower in sunshine, coming into its full bloom.

How do you know that your life is not a mistake but a unique expression of God's nature?

Charity

If anyone has material possessions and sees a brother or sister in need but has no pity on them, how can the love of God be in that person? Dear children, let us not love with words or speech but with actions and in truth.

1 JOHN 3:17-18 NIV

Christmas season is filled with opportunities to give. More so than during any other time of the year, charities offer venues for community service and vehicles for giving to others. In response, we drop money into buckets, tuck gifts under angel trees, and say extra prayers for those in need. In addition, we may find ourselves watering flowers for traveling neighbors or hosting a dinner party for those without family. Being a soft spot for those bruised souls in our path is a mark of discipleship.

Nobody wants to be alone or hungry on Christmas. Nobody wants to give their kids regretful hugs instead of gifts, shelter, or homemade food. In a time of hope and gladness, your active love reaches beyond the circumstances of the afflicted.

What opportunities do you have to give today?

FREE FOR LIFE

"Let any one of you who is without sin
be the first to throw a stone at her."

JOHN 8:7 NIV

If you feel Jesus is holding back his love and compassion from you because of something you have done or not done, think again! When Jesus died on the cross, he mercifully forgave you.

Forgiveness is only appropriate when someone has done something wrong, so God isn't hung up on your sin. Instead, God hung your sin on a cross and set you unequivocally free! Enjoy living.

What stones do people throw at you? How can you apply God's compassion in these situations?

KNOWN

They were saying to Him, "Where is Your Father?" Jesus answered,
"You know neither Me nor My Father; if you knew Me,
you would know My Father also."

JOHN 8:19 NASB

The Pharisees were taunting Jesus. They knew Joseph was only his step-father, and they threw his earthly status in his face. Why? Because he unraveled them. He unraveled them with his compassion, his love, and his willingness to associate with people they wouldn't touch. He didn't do things their way, and he called them out for being unholy. He didn't make sense to them, and he certainly didn't change to make them comfortable.

You're really not that different from Jesus. You are a stranger to this world, and because you inhabit it, all heaven breaks loose, and the earth gets set on its head. You might not see this for yourself, but it's true. That annoys some people as much as it blesses the rest. Take courage. Jesus understands you, sees you, and chooses to draw you even closer as you seek him.

In what ways are you encouraged to be more like Jesus?

ECHO GRATITUDE

Shout for joy to the LORD, all the earth.
Worship the LORD with gladness;
come before him with joyful songs.
Know that the LORD is God.
It is he who made us, and we are his;
we are his people, the sheep of his pasture.

PSALM 100:1-3 NIV

King David celebrates God. He worships him, gladly, singing songs to him. This sets David's heart in proper perspective. He knows who God is and what he has done for his people. David knows his identity through God, his Creator. He recognizes God's value and thereby his own.

When we encounter God's worthiness, we should experience gratitude, and echo that back to God. We can be overcome with God's goodness, his love, and his everlasting faithfulness.

What has God done lately that causes you to echo gratitude?

GOD PROVIDES

Then God said, "Behold, I have given you every plant yielding seed that is on the surface of all the earth, and every tree which has fruit yielding seed; it shall be food for you."

GENESIS 1:29 NASB

God gave us the first recursive gift: plants which bear seeds. He then told us to multiply and farm the land. In doing these two things, God provided for our food needs and took on the heavy lifting in turning seeds into food. He didn't do it for any reason beyond his love for each one of us.

We plant, we water, we weed, yet God creates the miracle. We can take delight in playing a very small part in our providence. Why? Because God loves to collaborate with us—and oftentimes what he wants to do is greater than we can ever imagine.

What seeds has God planted in your life lately?

EMOTIONS

There is an appointed time for everything.
And there is a time for every event under heaven.
A time to weep and a time to laugh;
A time to mourn and a time to dance.
A time to embrace and a time to shun embracing.
A time to be silent and a time to speak.
A time to love and a time to hate;
A time for war and a time for peace.

ECCLESIASTES 3:1, 4-8 NASB

God's emotions are on full display throughout Scripture. He has made us in his image. He understands our form, our emotions, and our frailties.

In his kindness, he gives Biblical instruction regarding how and why we handle emotion appropriately. He teaches us to express or conceal it, and to administer our responses in righteousness. What a loving God we have: that he would lead us into emotional strength and freedom.

How do you experience emotional strength?

MAKING CHOICES

> Out of the ground the LORD God caused to grow every tree that is pleasing to the sight and good for food; the tree of life also in the midst of the garden, and the tree of the knowledge of good and evil.
>
> GENESIS 2:9 NASB

God created the tree of life. He made all things, and he made all things good. He declared them good. So how was the tree of the knowledge of good and evil good? God gives us choices. Just like you can't make anyone love you, God won't try to make you love him or obey him. These are choices you make for yourself, and he designed this from the beginning.

Jesus wants us to bring him into every part of our beings, thus choosing life. As new creations, we have nothing left but to trust him, to judge what is good, and to do it.

How can you choose God again today?

Acceptance Lesson

*"I have brought you glory on earth by finishing the work
you gave me to do."*
JOHN 17:4 NIV

As we walk in love as faithful children, we will see fruit develop from what we do. We bring life and joy, truth and gentleness. We bring our gifts and ambitions. Often, this is met with delight and gratitude. Other times, people don't understand our intentions. Still other times, we sow our gifts faithfully, and never see good come of it. The gifts God gives us are a portion of a legacy that cannot be recognized in a generation. You may be feeding the poor, heartbroken there is not enough water. You may be clothing the naked, weeping that their bills won't be paid this month.

The point is this: you are being faithful. God is proud of you. And though the world around you may not understand what you are doing, and though you may not understand the world around you, Jesus has everything handled. He is making beautiful things in and with you. That is enough. Just walk with him in faith.

What good fruit is evident in your life right now?

TRiUNE GOD

In the beginning was the Word, and the Word was with God,
and the Word was God. He was in the beginning with God.

JOHN 1:1-2 NRSV

Have you ever opened a bar of chocolate and broke off one rectangle? That rectangle was surrounded by others that looked just like it. Each linked in with its mates to form a consolidated whole. Separately and collectively, the chocolate held the same essential properties throughout that gave it identity. One would consider this chocolate in terms of multiples or a whole, but the fact remained the same: it was all glorious chocolate.

God is a little like a chocolate bar. Whether he breaks off a piece that comes to earth, or enters the person who believes, it is very much true that if we have experienced him in some form, we have experienced the gracious Father who is seated on the throne of heaven. Each person of the Godhead is not at all a cookie cutter of the others, but these three persons agree completely, separately, and as one. They are—he is—God!

How else can you explain God as being three-in-one?

ETERNALLY BLESSED

How blessed is the man who fears the LORD,
Who greatly delights in His commandments.

PSALM 112:1 NASB

Blessings from God are gifts given as a result of his grace toward us. We can grow in God's graces just as we grow in the graces of the people around us. When we revere him and abide in his love, we naturally obey him from the heart. As our hearts knit together with God's, this grace improves.

The Lord keeps you steadfast, secure, and ultimately triumphant as you fear and obey him.

How do you feel you are growing in God's graces now?

FILLING THE HOLE

"Don't store up treasures here on earth where they can erode away or may be stolen. Store them in heaven where they will never lose their value and are safe from thieves. If your profits are in heaven, your heart will be there too."

MATTHEW 6:19-21 TLB

If asked, you could probably come up with several causes for temptation. Sooner or later, most people might gravitate toward blaming the devil for at least a few of their woes. But what about looking at ourselves? Sometimes we fill the void with whatever is handy: material objects, prestige, experiences, or relationships.

Have you ever thought about how that void grows more like an abyss every time you toss a new item into it? It is sobering. If we do not seek God at that opportunity, we try to plug the hole with distractions until we are lost in an endless sea of distress. Each believer is given Jesus and his Word, so we can navigate back to the only one who truly fills our souls.

What do you tend to fill your void with?
How can you let God be the one to fill it instead?

The Proper Time

"My dear Martha, you are worried and upset over all these details! There is only one thing worth being concerned about. Mary has discovered it, and it will not be taken away from her."

LUKE 10:41-42 NLT

Martha's problem was not that she was a hard worker but that she neglected the correct choice when it was laid before her. Hospitality is a great gift, and it will be useful to change your world. But right now, if God wants to speak with you personally, it is time to drop everything and listen. Sit at his feet, and let him provide for you as you have need.

Moses had a busy job as a shepherd. Yet, he stopped everything, one day, when he saw a burning bush. He could have just praised God as he walked along. Instead, he entered into a phenomenal partnership with God that changed the world.

How do you feel about this story of Mary and Martha?

DELIGHTED IN

The LORD directs the steps of the godly.
He delights in every detail of their lives.
Though they stumble, they will never fall,
for the LORD holds them by the hand.

PSALM 37:23-24 NLT

Jesus lives in you by choice. He has saved you quite capably. He is excited merely by being with you. Jesus doesn't need you to earn his gladness. He promises to calm your fears in his love.

God is so happy that you exist that the very joy of it causes him to burst forth into singing as he dances and twirls about you. You are encompassed and filled with God's no-holds-barred delight... in you.

Why do you think God delights in you?

Blessed Enemies

Feed your enemy if he is hungry. If he is thirsty give him something to drink and you will be "heaping coals of fire on his head." In other words, he will feel ashamed of himself for what he has done to you.

ROMANS 12:20 TLB

Amongst nomadic and rural populations, fire remains essential to survival. If someone's fire goes out, they must scurry to the stoop of a neighbor. Clay pot balanced on her head, she hopes for life-giving fire. If the neighbor loves her, she will heap hot coals into that jar, and the household will be saved.

God says his goodness brings people to repentance. They feel shame at the disparity between their motives and people who give them mercy. For this reason—for mercy and reconciliation—we heap up unlikely kindness on the very ones who hurt us. We leave that kindness as a jewel in Jesus' hand: a token that softens hearts where needed. As the flames of mercy spring up for a cold heart, we steal death from the enemy, and create opportunities for reconciliation and peace.

Who are the people in your life you need to bless today?

Illuminated Motives

A plan in the heart of a man is like deep water,
But a man of understanding draws it out.

PROVERBS 20:5 NASB

Sometimes we fail to understand people's motives. They get in our faces, grate on our nerves, and disrupt our peace. In fact, we can, at times, question their authenticity. The Bible says you will need understanding to figure people out.

Wisdom means knowing what to do, and understanding means knowing why. According to the Word, you ask, read the Bible, and pay attention to what happens around you in order to make strides in both. Be pure-hearted and receptive as you pursue, and you will learn a great deal. You will discover what questions to ask yourself and others to get to the root of a motive.

What has God shared with you lately?

UNRESERVEDLY

David asked, "Is there anyone still left of the house of Saul
to whom I can show kindness for Jonathan's sake?"

2 SAMUEL 9:1 NIV

In the story of David, we meet an infirmed grandchild of Saul named
Mephibosheth. Because of Saul's cruelty to David, Mephibosheth would
have been an unlikely candidate for David's favor. David had the heart
of God, though. For the sake of his friend, Jonathan, David granted
Mephibosheth a regular seat at his table as well as his grandfather's
entire estate and the servants he needed. David extended luxurious favor
upon one who could not possibly benefit him, and who did not think
himself a friend.

It is true: God is quizzically kind and compassionate to all people,
regardless of how they stand with him. Although you may feel you have
let God down, or you have little to offer, Jesus invites you to his feast table
every day. He welcomes you to stay in his presence so you will enjoy the
lavish care he continually gives you.

How can you extend God's kindness to others today?

Properly Dressed

Put on the new self, created to be like God in true righteousness and holiness.

EPHESIANS 4:24 NIV

You have such a beautiful future ahead of you! What a blessing it is that you will affect people by just being you: lovely, holy, and loved of God. Because you are a child of God, your home isn't here. It's in heaven, where spiritual weather is always fine. If you go out into an earthly storm, you change your inward clothes to meet the earthly challenges before you.

Earth isn't your home turf; life here is laden with storms. Fortunately, Christ has given you ample covering for the weather. Put on the new man to overcome with Christ. He has offered it to you, and he finds it precious that you wear the clothing he provides.

How can you dress yourself for the weather of life?

As You Are

God chose what is foolish in the world to shame the wise; God chose what is weak in the world to shame the strong; God chose what is low and despised in the world, even things that are not, to bring to nothing things that are, so that no human being might boast in the presence of God.

1 CORINTHIANS 1:27-29 ESV

When Christ gathered his dream team for spreading the good news across the globe, he prayerfully selected young and inexperienced men who had nothing to recommend them. He sidestepped experienced people to fill the role with someone who would need to trust him and listen closely in order to succeed. Matthew was a customs official, but Jesus charged Judas with taking care of finances. In Acts, Jesus called Gentile Peter to convert and serve the Jews, while Pharisee Paul was sent to the Gentiles.

Even today, God has this principle: he is so pleased with you walking in his trust that he uses you to make his name great in unlikely places—often where you cannot go in your own strength. Trust him to tell you where and to guide you as you go.

Why did God choose you?

BOLDLY PROCLAIM

They hurried off and found Mary and Joseph, and the baby, who was lying in the manger. When they had seen him, they spread the word concerning what had been told them about this child, and all who heard it were amazed at what the shepherds said to them.

LUKE 2:16-18 NIV

When the shepherds were told about Jesus, they didn't pencil him into their schedules; they ran to him. They ran as fast as their feet could carry them. Who watched over the sheep? Who knows? But in that moment, they knew the importance of the Lord's advent, and they rushed to Bethlehem, and into his barn stall, to see him. Once they saw him, and experienced him, they rushed to tell of him. God didn't choose earthly leaders to spread the word. He chose messengers who would faithfully carry the good news.

Who is this Lord of ours, that fishermen and ranch hands spread his good news? Hallelujah! Christ has come. Tell your friends. Tell your neighbors. Tell everyone you meet. Jesus is the Lord, and he has come in the flesh. Hallelujah!

What can you boldly proclaim about God today?

Christmas song

"The Root of Jesse will spring up, one who will arise to rule over the nations; in him the Gentiles will hope." May the God of hope fill you with all joy and peace as you trust in him, so that you may overflow with hope by the power of the Holy Spirit.

ROMANS 15:12-13 NIV

Jesus, a Jew, came so all people would be qualified to experience his indescribable hope, joy, and peace as they placed their faith in him. It's not a wonder that a great band of angels joined together in praise that night. Jesus is the true basis for every believer's hope and joy, for this season and for all time.

You may be alone today or with many people. You may be reading this Christmas day, or you may be catching up after a flurry of activity. Perhaps you are flipping through this book, and you've stopped on this passage. Wherever you are, and whatever your circumstance, you have a gift from the Lord for this very day. It's okay; a Christmas gift from God doesn't expire! The gift God has for you, each and every day, is this: he is your strength and your song. And he always will be.

What is your Christmas song?

No Returns

God never changes his mind about the people he calls
and the things he gives them.

ROMANS 11:29 NCV

The days and weeks after Christmas can be an awkward mess. In one instance or another, we find we've given or have been given a gift that is unsuitable or wrongly sized. We may have overlooked someone entirely. The recipient may stand in line at a store for a return or write a letter of thanks for something that, at best, caused a moment of humor.

Isn't it refreshing that God, in his great understanding and thoughtfulness, gives gifts appropriate to us: gifts that do not cause regret? Moreover, these often produce gifts we give to the world, and back to God.

What has God entrusted to you that you've thought too big to handle? What will you do, today, to begin the journey?

Freed from Anger

People with understanding control their anger;
a hot temper shows great foolishness.
PROVERBS 14:29 NLT

We've all snapped. We must be wise in our anger, though, because it may destroy the protections God has built into our lives. Anger is a response to suppressed fear, humiliation, rejection, or pain. Getting to the root of these events allows us to deal with anger, disarm, and move forward, unencumbered. Jesus isn't cruel: he doesn't want you to be mishandled. He will reward you as you submit to him, responsively, in times of both peace and injustice.

Wrath is vengeful anger which retaliates rather than reconciles. We thwart the devil by casting wrath, anger, vengefulness, and bitterness from our hearts and choosing kindness, tenderheartedness, and forgiveness.

Where have you allowed anger to grip you?
Can you let God bring peace instead?

Steadfast Hope

We know that in all things God works for the good of those who love
him, who have been called according to his purpose.

ROMANS 8:28 NIV

Not everything starts out being God's idea for your life, but he makes
beautiful things of it, in spite of that. The good God has in mind might
not even be on your radar yet. But if the love of God is peaceable and
kind, then surely his gifts are in step with that.

Sometimes, it is hard to imagine life being good after our world gets
swayed. True to form, God is faithful in the midst of it, and he has plans
that defy your expectations. Take comfort, and choose to hope for the
future and for your good.

How do you know that God is working in you?

SOURCE OF BEAUTY

Do not adorn yourselves outwardly by braiding your hair, and by wearing gold ornaments or fine clothing; rather, let your adornment be the inner self with the lasting beauty of a gentle and quiet spirit, which is very precious in God's sight.

1 PETER 3:3-4 NRSV

"Pretty is as pretty does," women often tell their girls. Why? Because curling our hair, buying trifles, and improving clothing, posture, and speech isn't where beauty is found. Jesus coaches us in beauty. Peers and magazine articles address our appearances, distracting from the valuable person within.

Beauty shines from within. It dresses in humility and true wisdom. It grows in an environment of reverent, holy living, thriving in worship and glorifying God. It is embodied in Christ and his heart toward people. It is good to look nice, and sometimes our gifts or calling require it. But we need to keep holiness our central focus as we offer our appearance to God. We are meant to be adorned with his beauty.

What does God find truly beautiful about you?

FIRST FRUITS

The Holy Spirit also witnesses to us; for after He had said before,
"This is the covenant that I will make with them after those days,
says the LORD: I will put My laws into their hearts,
and in their minds I will write them."

HEBREWS 10:15-16 NKJV

In the original Passover, the Festival of Shelters, the nation of Israel celebrated receiving the law. It was day fifty since they stepped foot out of Egypt, and they had seen mighty things at God's hand. As God handed Moses the law, he also told him that one day it would be written on people's hearts. Year after year, the Israelites celebrated this day by bringing in the first fruits of their fields: grain.

The year Christ was crucified at Passover, the disciples and followers of Jesus were gathered in the upper room. The promised Holy Spirit came and filled them, thus writing the law of the Spirit in their hearts. True to form, the first fruits of the harvest were brought in that day when three thousand souls converted at Peter's admonition to repent and be baptized.

What first fruits do you have to give back to God?

LOAD OF ANXIETY

Always be full of joy in the Lord; I say it again, rejoice! Let everyone see that you are unselfish and considerate in all you do. Remember that the Lord is coming soon. Don't worry about anything; instead, pray about everything; tell God your needs, and don't forget to thank him for his answers.

PHILIPPIANS 4:4-6 TLB

Carrying anxiety is like over-packing a car for a trip. Gas mileage suffers, companions have a hard time joining you, and blocked vision endangers your car and others on the road. Clearly, you need to unpack anxiety in order to free yourself for a better journey. So, what is the key to shaking anxiety from your life? Rejoice in God, and gratefully request his help with your encumbrances.

Fortunately, joy in the Lord is available in all circumstances. It's that jug of lemonade in your fridge which readily fills your cup. Rejoicing produces refreshment. Your problems become manageable because Jesus is invited into all areas of your life. He is your accompanying reality—anxiety can no longer take that seat.

How can you let go of anxiety and trust God in the coming year?